MODERN STITCHERY

STITCHES, PATTERNS, FREE-FORM DESIGNING

by B. Kay Fraser

CROWN PUBLISHERS, INC., NEW YORK

ACKNOWLEDGMENT

The author would like to express her appreciation to The Eugene Stitcher's Guild of Eugene, Oregon, which contributed a wide variety of designs and ideas to this book

Inquiries should be addressed to Crown Publishers, Inc., 419 Park Avenue South, New York, N.Y. 10016.

Printed in the United States of America
Published simultaneously in Canada by
General Publishing Company Limited

Library of Congress Cataloging in Publication Data

Fraser, B. Kay
  Modern stitchery.

  Includes index.
  1. Embroidery.   I.   Title.
TT770.F66   1976   746.4′4   75-28078
ISBN 0-517-51864-3
ISBN 0-517-51865-1 pbk.

CONTENTS

ONE

INTRODUCTION

What is modern stitchery? An easy yet challenging needlecraft that enables you to create wall hangings, decorate linens and clothing, make unique pillows, personalize jewelry, and add colorful designs to every household item made of fabric.

Best yet, if you can thread a needle, you can stitch! With instructions given in this book, stitchery may be as easy as a paint-by-number kit. You simply use a needle as you would a brush, use fabric as a canvas, and use patterns to tell you where to stitch. So even beginners can create professional-looking stitchery.

But modern stitchery also presents a challenge to more experienced needlecraftsmen. The endless choice of stitches, color combinations, and unusual designs keep stitchery from becoming ho-hum. It is as simple or as complex a craft as you care to make it!

Perhaps stitchery's versatility as well as its warmth and beauty is what makes this hobby so popular. Almost every woman's home or craft magazine features stitchery projects. Stitchery kits are prominently displayed in craft and variety stores and in the sewing sections of department stores.

However, these projects are called by several names: crewel embroidery, yarn embroidery, creative stitchery, jiffy stitchery, and so forth.

Actually, modern stitchery is a rebirth of crewel embroidery, which became fashionable in England during the seventeenth century at the time of James I, or the Jacobean era. At that time crewel wool (a fine loosely twisted 2-ply wool yarn) was used to stitch elaborate copied designs, most often on bedspreads, upholstery, and clothing. Designs usually featured exotic trees, birds, animals, and flowers—objects that were meaningful to stitchers of long ago. Often the shades of only one color were used, such as blue or green; and one major stitch called the crewel stitch was used. (Today we call this stitch the stem stitch.)

Although modern stitchery has its roots in crewel embroidery, the work done today is much quicker, more imaginative, less delicate, and much more colorful. We are no longer limited to crewel yarn, but can use washable acrylics, rug yarn, macramé cord, and even kite string. We can expand fabric selection from white linen to rough burlap, pillow ticking, homespun cotton, and brightly colored synthetic linens. We can incorporate traditional stitches with techniques from Asia and Europe and even invent our own stitches. And we can stitch any design imaginable—be it Van Gogh's *Sunflowers*, a simple owl or mushroom, a wild free-form design, or a treasured memory such as a child's favorite toy, a blueprint of your home, or your favorite vacation scene.

This is why many of today's stitchers no longer wish to call their craft simply "embroidery." It is not as tedious as the original crewel embroidery nor is it as limited as simply filling in stitches on a stamped design, which became popular after World War II. It has evolved into a craft that is bounded only by your imagination.

In fact, modern stitchery is often considered an art form in the same way as oil painting. Fortunately, stitchery does not always require the talent or originality of oil painting, although you may be surprised at the hidden talents stitchery can bring out in you!

Whether you are an experienced stitcher or a beginner with ten thumbs, this book can help you discover your talent. You can create any stitchery project in four easy steps. The following four chapters explain these steps with easy-to-follow instructions and illustrations. The remaining chapters show instructions, patterns, and photographs of completed stitchery projects that were made by following the four steps.

You may re-create these projects or use them for inspiration. The important thing is to start stitching! Not only will you discover a relaxing, rewarding hobby, but your handiwork will create warm colorful designs that can be displayed with pride in your home or given with special meaning to friends.

Modern stitchery features colorful yarn and creative designs that even a beginner can stitch. Stitching by Sherri Gorman, design by Sunset Designs. Available in kit form at art needlework and department stores.

TWO

STEP ONE...
GATHER MATERIALS

Materials needed for stitchery are few and inexpensive. Most supplies can be found in the sewing section of department and variety stores. The best selection of supplies, however, is often in art needlework shops. (Look under Art Needlework in the Yellow Pages for locations.) If you live in an area where shops are scarce, write for free craft supply catalogs from:

Merribee
2904 West Lancaster
P.O. Box 9680
Fort Worth, Texas 76107

LeeWards Creative Crafts, Inc.
1200 St. Charles Road
Elgin, Illinois 60120

Basically, you will need fabric, yarn, needles and scissors, and hoop or frame, which are discussed in detail below. You may also purchase stitchery kits that contain most materials needed. Completing a kit is an excellent way for beginners to build up confidence in their stitchery abilities. Do read this book before selecting a kit so that you will be able to make a wiser choice of kits and make any changes or corrections.

FABRIC

You may use any fabric for stitchery that is strong, loosely woven, and not so nubbly that it will interfere with the stitch. Favorite fabrics are linens, synthetic linen weaves, burlap, hopsacking, tie interfacing, and twill weave wool.

Fabrics to be avoided are knits and stretchy materials that will lose their shape; heavily textured materials such as terry cloth that will pull on the yarn as you stitch; and tightly woven materials such as poplin and gingham that will pucker when yarn is pulled through. (Tighter weaves may be used if you substitute embroidery floss for yarn.) If you are not familiar with fabrics, just ask the clerk to suggest suitable materials.

When selecting fabric, think of it as the background (or canvas) for your stitchery picture. Would a colored background enhance the design or swallow it? Would a rough fabric complement the design or would a smooth texture be more appropriate? Will the fabric receive hard wear and should therefore be strong and washable? Whenever in doubt, you will never go wrong with a white linen weave.

Because few projects require more than half a yard of fabric, your investment is only a dollar or two. But you can cut corners even more by buying remnants, using leftover fabric from other projects, and recycling old clothes. Colored burlap, often used for other crafts, may be used if you wash it first—otherwise the color may fade.

A wide selection of loosely woven fabric suitable for stitchery is found in department, fabric, and art needlework stores.

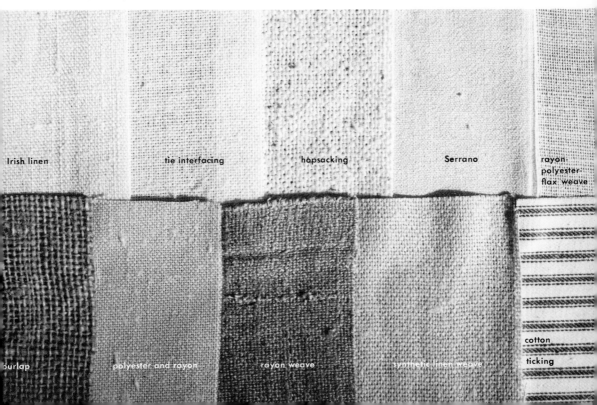

Irish linen   tie interfacing   hopsacking   Serrano   rayon-polyester-flax weave

burlap   polyester and rayon   rayon weave   synthetic linen weave   cotton ticking

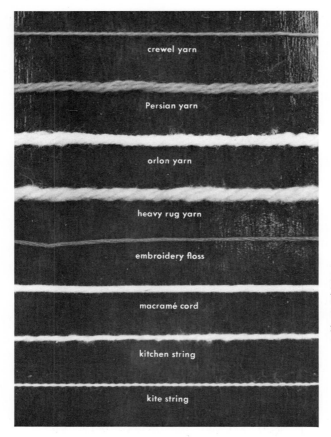

crewel yarn

Persian yarn

orlon yarn

heavy rug yarn

embroidery floss

macramé cord

kitchen string

kite string

Persian wool is a popular yarn for stitchery; but any type of yarn, thread, floss, string, etc., may be used including the types shown.

YARN

Yarn most often used in stitchery kits and preferred by beginners is 3-ply Persian yarn. Available in art needlework shops and through craft catalogs, Persian yarn is sturdy (won't fray or break), economical (a dozen small skeins for under $4), and offers endless color combinations (over 240 shades available).

But the joy of modern stitchery is that you are not confined to any one type of yarn. You may use heavy rug yarn, cotton yarn, baby fine yarn, macramé cord, crewel yarn, twine, embroidery floss, acrylic yarn. In other words, select any yarn whose color and texture appeal to you.

Keep in mind that the yarn must pull through the fabric without puckering. As an example, burlap is loosely woven and therefore a coarse heavy yarn could be used. Denim or muslin, being more tightly woven, would be more suitable for embroidery floss.

If you wish to have a yarn supply on hand, select small skeins or cards of:

white	tan	purple	dark green	gold
black	rust	dark blue	medium green	orange
gray	red	light blue	yellow green	
brown	pink	turquoise	yellow	

This selection covers the neutral and primary colors with variations for shading. When selecting colors for a specific project, however, let Mother Nature be your guide. For example, daffodils will be yellow, apples red, leaves green, trees brown, and so forth. Or, you may choose a dominant color to blend with room decor, such as orange. Then fill in the rest of the design with accent colors that coordinate or contrast with orange, such as gold and green.

Color schemes may also be copied from the color section of this book. But the very best color guide is your own eye; if a color looks good to you, use it!

NEEDLES AND SCISSORS

Crewel needles are most suitable for stitchery. These needles are short, about 1¾ inches, and have long slender eyes to accommodate several strands of yarn. Sharp-pointed crewel needles also enable you to "stab" the fabric and pull the yarn without ruining the weave of the fabric. Crewel needles come in sizes 1 to 12, with the largest number actually being the smallest needle. A size 3 or 4 will complete most projects, although the size of the needle will be dictated by the weight of the yarn and weave of the fabric you are using.

In other words, select a needle that will make a hole large enough in the fabric for the yarn to come through. Too small a needle will strip the yarn and too large a needle will leave half-filled holes.

For example, if you are using embroidery floss on denim, you could use a size 10 crewel embroidery needle. If you are using heavy rug yarn, you could use a size 1 crewel needle or even a tapestry needle. A tapestry (or yarn) needle has a big eye, blunt point, and works well with heavy yarns, raffia, or twine that is being stitched onto loosely woven fabric.

Select an assortment of good quality needles and experiment to see which works best. Keep needles sharp by placing them in an emery cushion when not in use.

Scissors are also an indispensable item as you stitch, but you may use any sharp scissors already in your home. Small long-pointed embroidery scissors are particularly handy while stitching, and long fabric shears are ideal for cutting fabric.

Thimbles are optional. Some stitchers find thimbles a nuisance and others cannot work without them. A metal thimble that fits your finger snugly is most satisfactory.

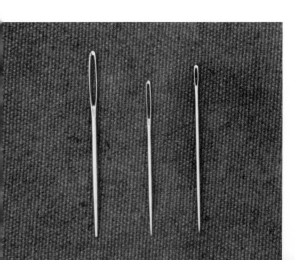

Frequently used needles for modern stitchery are (*from left to right*) a yarn or tapestry needle, a crewel needle, and an embroidery needle.

HOOPS AND STRETCHERS

Embroidery hoops or needlework stretchers are often used in modern stitchery to hold the fabric taut while you stitch. This ensures a smoother, more accurate stitch.

Hoops range in size from 4 to 10 inches, and the most satisfactory hoops may be tightened once the fabric is inserted. If you do not presently own an embroidery hoop, select a 6- or 8-inch wooden hoop with an adjustable screw.

To use a hoop, place the inner circle on a flat surface and lay the fabric over it. (The fabric should be at least 2 inches larger than the hoop.) Place the outer circle on top of the fabric and press down so that the fabric fits snugly between the inner and outer circles. Pull the fabric taut on all sides keeping the grain straight. Tighten screw.

Hoops are handy because they are small and may be stashed in a plastic bag or workbasket with fabric and yarns so that you may stitch any time, any place. However, hoops have the drawback of crumpling fabric; isolating a small section of the design so you cannot see "the whole picture"; and require more handling so that the fabric may become soiled. So, if you are stitching a large design, remove the hoop after each use to prevent wrinkling and spread the design out to see "the whole picture."

Stretchers are often used instead of hoops on larger designs. Needlework stretchers are merely four thin strips of wood that may be adjusted to fit the fabric. You can make your own stretcher; find one at the art needlework store; or use an adjustable artist's canvas stretcher found in art supply stores.

To make a stretcher, buy wooden strips or laths from the lumber supply yard, cut to the desired size with a saw, and nail the sides together. (Homemade stretchers may also be used as a frame for the completed stitchery.)

Fabric is held in place on the stretcher by the use of pushpins, tacks, or staples. Tacks are usually placed at about 1-inch intervals to hold fabric taut without distorting the weave. The stretcher is normally placed in your lap to stitch and braced against a table or counter. Even if you use an embroidery hoop while stitching, you may wish to tack the fabric to a stretcher when completed in order to stretch the fabric back into shape.

Still another idea is to select a wooden picture frame as your stretcher. Simply lay the frame face down on top of the fabric. Pull the fabric to the back of the frame and tack or staple. When the stitchery is finished, remove the tacks and mount inside the frame. (More about framing in Chapter 5.)

Advanced and beginning stitchers might also consider the purchase of a floor model needlework stand. In effect, this stand aids the serious stitcher as an easel aids an artist.

However, some stitchers prefer to stitch freehand. They find hoops

Embroidery hoops hold fabric taut while you stitch.

Needlework stretchers may be adjusted to accommodate most designs and keep the entire design distortion-free as you stitch.

Homemade stretchers are easy to make with wood laths cut to size, nails, and hammer.

and stretchers awkward. Others prefer a hoop for flat stitches, no hoop for raised stitches, and a stretcher for final blocking. Experiment to see which device works best for you.

THREE

STEP TWO...
CREATE OR COPY
A DESIGN

Anything you can see, you can stitch! You can make seascapes, spring bouquets, animal scenes, fanciful mushrooms and owls, lovable children, Indian designs, folk art flowers, religious scenes, wedding and anniversary mementos, great artists' masterpieces, and bright fruits and vegetables.

DESIGN SOURCES

Before stitching a design, of course, you must first work out the design, or pattern, on paper. If you are adept at freehand drawing, you can simply draw the design on paper with a pencil.

If you are not adept at drawing, do not despair. There are many excellent sources of designs available that you can copy. For example, you can copy tole painting designs, color book designs, embroidery patterns, designs found in this book, art posters, watercolor and oil painting pictures, needlepoint designs, wallpaper and fabric patterns, china and silver patterns, and favorite photographs. Often women's magazines feature stitchery designs. And magazine and newspaper advertisements are a gold mine of designs.

To copy a design, you merely use tracing paper and a soft-leaded pencil, such as a #2. Place the tracing paper over the design (you may wish to hold it in place with masking tape) and copy. If the design is on wood or canvas, use a light touch so that you will not damage the original design.

You may adapt any design to stitchery by tracing over it with tracing paper and a pencil.

ENLARGING OR REDUCING DESIGNS

Sometimes the design will be too large or small for your needs. If so, you may take the design to a blueprint or printing shop and ask them to reduce or enlarge it for a few dollars. Or, you may photograph the design and have the photography shop enlarge the picture to the desired size.

The quickest and easiest method, however, is to square off the pattern. Using a ruler, draw proportioned squares on top of the original design as shown. Then draw proportionately larger or smaller squares on another piece of paper and fill in the design, square by square. For example, if your design is small and you wish to enlarge it, draw lines ¼ inch apart on the original design. Then draw lines 1 inch apart on another piece of paper, and draw in the design.

You may simplify this technique even further by buying graph paper, which is already printed in squares.

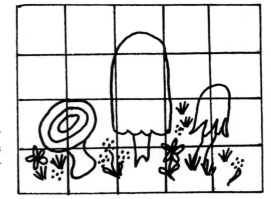

Designs may be enlarged or reduced by squaring off the original design, then filling in squares that are correspondingly larger or smaller.

TRANSFERRING DESIGNS TO FABRIC

By transferring your design to fabric, you make your stitchery as easy as a paint-by-number kit. Experienced stitchers often draw the pattern directly on the fabric with chalk or pencil (using light pressure in case the mark may need to be erased).

Designs are easily transferred to fabric with the use of an iron-on transfer pencil.

A design in a newspaper advertisement was adapted to stitchery by first squaring off the design to enlarge it, then using a transfer pencil to put the design on fabric. Stitchery by Skip McGarvery.

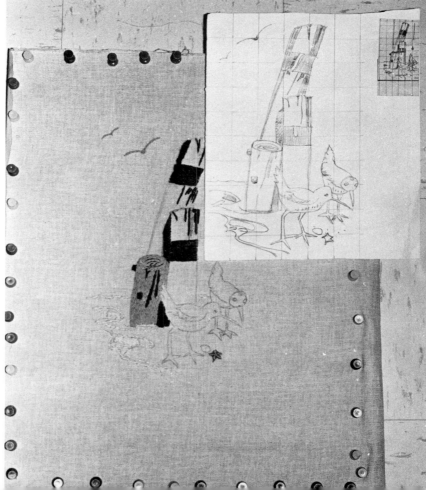

Beginners, however, will find it easier to use one of these three transfer methods:

Dressmaker's carbon method. Using a dressmaker's carbon kit (or graphite paper from art stores), first place the design over the fabric exactly where you want it to be. Secure with pins or masking tape. Then slip the carbon paper, sticky side down, between the fabric and design. Trace over the design with a soft pencil or tracing wheel and the design will be transferred to the fabric. (Some regular office-type carbon paper may be used with caution—but it does smudge much more easily than dressmaker's carbon.)

Transfer pencil method. Purchase a hot-iron transfer pencil from a needlework shop or art store. These pencils enable you to transfer a design in two easy steps. First trace over the back side of the paper pattern with the transfer pencil. (Some colored pencils work as well as transfer pencils.) Then place the pattern, pencil side down, onto the fabric and iron on low heat. Use a light and quick touch with the iron, placing it on one area at a time—do not slide the iron.

Back tracing method. Turn your pattern to the reverse side and trace all lines with a soft leaded pencil or carpenter's pencil. Then tape or pin the design, right side up, on the fabric. Using a pencil or sharp point, such as a knitting needle, trace the design once again. The pressure should transfer the pencil markings onto the fabric.

FOUR

STEP THREE...
SELECT THE
STITCHES

Now comes the fun of deciding which stitches you will use to complete your design. There are hundreds of stitches to choose from ... or you can invent your own. Even the most common stitches can be varied by the tension of your stitch, by the number of strands used, and by the length or slant of the stitch.

But basically all stitches can be categorized in about half a dozen stitch families. Stitches here are grouped according to similarities in methods used to make the stitch. (Some stitches are composites and can fit in more than one family.) These families and the most popular stitches in each group are illustrated on the following pages.

Note that stitches are usually named for their place of origin, such as Romanian stitch; for the way they look, such as satin stitch or herringbone stitch; or for the way they are worked, such as backstitch or needle weaving stitch.

Beginners will be attracted to the flat stitch group because they look and are so easy. And a very nice picture can result from using just two or three stitches from this group. But no stitch is difficult. Practice a stitch once or twice on scrap fabric before using it on your design to prove to yourself just how easy most stitches are.

Browse through the stitches shown and notice the way they are used in the completed projects shown in the following chapters. Then decide which stitches best suit the items in your design. For example, the fishbone stitch makes very nice leaves. The lazy daisy stitch is perfect for small flowers. A needle weaving stitch is excellent for baskets. A series of French knots make a fanciful mushroom cap. The satin stitch is dandy for smooth flower petals and ladybugs. The stem stitch makes a smooth outline, and the chevron stitch an intriguing border. A looped stem stitch creates realistic animal fur.

Choose the stitch that best creates the effect you want. Then, using your paper pattern as a guide, write the name of the stitch on or by the item where it will be used. You may also wish to write the color of the yarn you have decided upon.

If desired, beginners may wish to stitch a sampler using all the stitches shown here. A sampler not only provides good practice, but it demonstrates to beginners how easy the stitches are and may be used as a reference for all future projects. (See Chapter 7 for sampler ideas.) Or, stitch the mushroom design shown to learn the five most commonly used stitches. (Please see Chapter 5 for important tips before actual stitching begins.)

Use your pattern as a guide by writing down the stitches and colors selected. Your stitchery is now as easy as a paint-by-number kit!

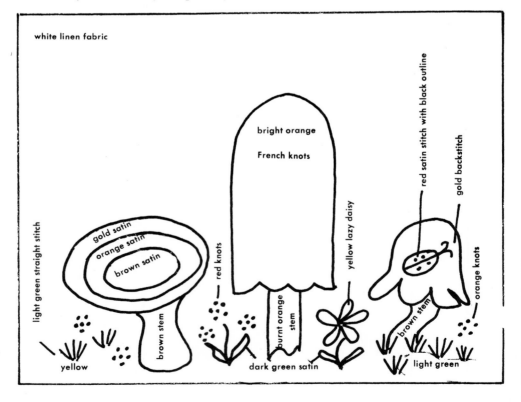

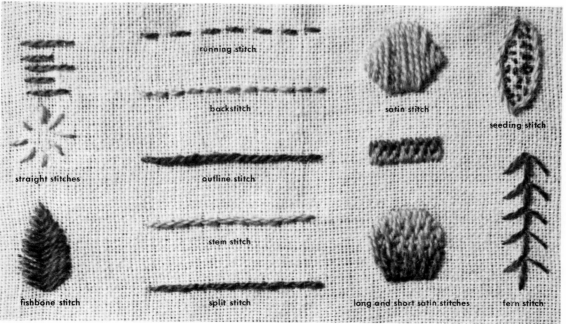

Flat stitches

FLAT STITCHES*

Straight Stitch

Straight stitches may be worked in any direction and any length, but never over curved lines. Bring the needle up at 1, down at 2, up at 3, etc., until the design is complete.

Seeding Stitch

Seeding stitches are many tiny straight stitches worked in any direction. Stitches should be of equal length.

Satin Stitch

The most popular of filling stitches, the satin stitch is actually many straight stitches laid side by side without overlapping until the desired area is completely covered with thread. Bring needle up at 1, in at 2, out at 3 until completed. Keep edges neat.

Long and Short Stitch

This stitch is worked the same as the satin stitch except stitches are alternately long and short. After one row is completed, the next

---

* If you are left-handed, you may find the diagrams easier to follow by turning them upside down and then following the numbers.

row is generally worked in a different color to provide shading. On the second row, use long stitches where short stitches were used in the first row and vice versa.

Running Stitch

Working from right to left, insert needle up at 1, down at 2, up at 3. Pick up an equal amount of cloth each time.

Backstitch

Working from right to left, bring needle up a short distance to left of point where line will start(1). Then insert needle a short distance to the right(2), and bring needle out a short distance to left(3) of starting point. Keep equal distances between points 1, 2, and 3 for an even looking stitch.

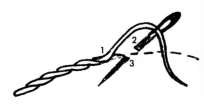

Outline Stitch

The outline stitch is just the opposite of the backstitch, being worked from left to right. Also, at point 3, the needle is inserted slightly below points 1 and 2; and the thread is always kept *above* the needle. The final effect is a completely covered line that looks well on curved lines.

Stem Stitch

The most popular outlining stitch is the stem stitch (also called the crewel stitch), which also looks well as filling when rows of stem stitch are worked side by side. The stem stitch is worked the same as the outline stitch except that the thread is held *below* the needle instead of above. Try to keep an equal distance between points 1, 2, and 3.

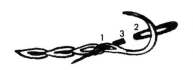

Split Stitch

The split stitch is handy for tiny lines and stems. It resembles a fine chain stitch, but is worked quite differently. Make a straight stitch coming up at 1 and down at 2. Then come up in the center at point 3, splitting the thread exactly in the center. Continue working from left to right. Point 3 will become the starting point for your next stitch.

Fern Stitch

The fern stitch is three straight stitches of equal length starting from the same central point(1). Bring yarn out at 1, in at 2, out at 1, in at 3, out at 1, in at 4. To continue the design, bring needle back out at 5, which becomes the starting point for the next stitches.

Fishbone Stitch

This stitch is useful for filling small shapes such as leaves and may be worked open (with fabric showing between stitches) or closed (with fabric completely covered by thread). Bring needle out at 1, in at 2, out at 3, in at 4, out at 5. Repeat until shape is filled, keeping edges even and stitches sloping.

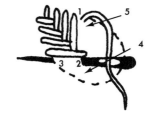

LOOPED STITCHES

Lazy Daisy Stitch

A favorite stitch for making small flower petals, the lazy daisy is easily completed by bringing the needle up at 1, in at 2 (right next to 1), and out at 3. Making sure thread is under the needle, pull the thread through. Go in at 4, which makes a small stitch to hold the loop in place. Continue making lazy daisy stitches until the flower is completed.

Looped stitches

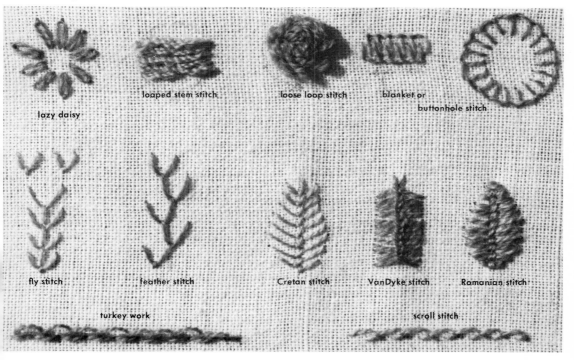

lazy daisy

looped stem stitch

loose loop stitch

blanket or
buttonhole stitch

fly stitch

feather stitch

Cretan stitch

VanDyke stitch

Ramanian stitch

turkey work

scroll stitch

Blanket or Buttonhole Stitch

Working from left to right, the blanket stitch is made by bringing the needle up at 1, then in at 2, and out at 3 before pulling the thread through. Point 3 is now your starting point for the next stitch. This stitch is effective as borders, for small flowers, or as a finish for the raw edges of appliqué. When these stitches are placed side by side as closely as possible, they are called buttonhole stitches.

Fly Stitch

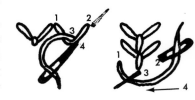

Also called a Y-stitch, this stitch is similar to the lazy daisy except points 1 and 2 are farther apart. Pull needle through at 1, then in at 2, and out at 3, forming a loop under the needle before pulling through. The stitch is secured by going in at 4, which may be a long or short stitch. The fly stitch may be attached vertically by making the securing stitch the same length as the side stitches.

Feather Stitch

A dainty stitch for foliage or filling small areas, the feather stitch is worked from top to bottom and is similar to the fly stitch except that no securing stitch is used. Bring needle through at top center(1), then in at 2 and out at 3, keeping yarn under the needle. Pull through. Next, insert needle at 4 and out at 5, keeping yarn below needle. Pull through and repeat sequence. Note that stitches 1 and 2 are directly across from each other and that stitch 3 is actually the starting point for the next stitch.

Cretan Stitch

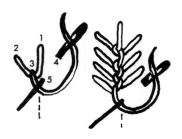

The Cretan stitch is similar to the fly stitch except that the stitches are worked much closer together, which creates a plait down the center. This stitch may be worked side by side or with spaces between stitches. Stitches are usually slanting. Pull needle through at 1, in at 2, and out at 3, keeping yarn under needle. Pull through. Then go in at 4 and out at 5, keeping yarn under needle. Pull through.

Continue alternating stitches from side to side until design is completed.

Romanian Stitch

This stitch may also be worked open or closed and stitches may be straight or slanting. It is similar to the fly and lazy daisy stitches except that points 1 and 2 are directly across from each other. Bring needle out at 1, in at 2, and out at 3. Pull through. Secure stitch by inserting needle below the yarn (4) and slightly to the left of point 3. Pull needle through at 5 and repeat sequence. The securing stitch thus forms a plait down the center.

VanDyke Stitch

This stitch also has a middle plait, only the plait is created by passing the needle under the yarn. Pull the yarn through at 1 and then take a small stitch at 2 and go in at 3. Pull the yarn through again at 4, then pass the needle under the crossed threads from left to right before inserting at 5. Try not to pull stitches too tightly or the center plait will not be even.

Scroll Stitch

Useful for outlining, borders, and tendrils, the scroll stitch is worked from left to right. Pull needle through at 1, then insert at 2, and bring out at 3 (a slanting stitch). Before pulling needle through, make a loop below the needle. Hold yarn between points 1 and 2 with thumb while pulling needle through so yarn will stay taut. Point 3 is now the starting point for the next stitch. Space stitches evenly.

Turkey Work

This unusual stitch is handy for textured effects, such as fur or feathers. Bring needle through at 1, then in at 2, and out at 3 (a backstitch). Keep yarn *below* needle and pull yarn flat to fabric. Now, go in at 4 and pull out at 2, leaving a loop *above* needle. The stitch is repeated by going in at 5 and out at 4, thus alternating between backstitches and

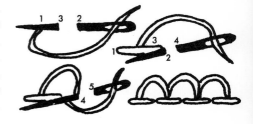

loops. Keep stitches an equal distance apart and loops an equal length.

Loose Loop Stitch

This stitch may be used for fur or flower centers and may be clipped when completed. Bring the needle through at 1, then in at 2, and back out at 1. Pull through leaving a loop about ¼ inch high. Then insert needle in at 3 and out at 4, which anchors the loop. Hold loop with thumb so it will not be pulled through while making stitches 3 and 4. Point 4 now becomes the starting point for the next stitch.

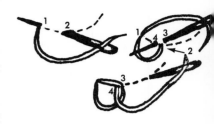

Looped Stem Stitch

This stitch is worked from left to right and is similar to the stem stitch except that a loop of thread is left between points 2 and 3. Go in at 1, leaving a small tail. Come out at 2 and in at 3, then out at 1, splitting the yarn as you come up. Pull through. Repeat going in at 4 and up at 3, again splitting the yarn and leaving a loop. Keep stitches an equal distance and keep loops similar in size. Worked in rows side by side, this stitch is excellent for creating "fur." When making fur, keep stitches about ⅛ inch apart and loops about ¼ inch high. If desired, stitches may be clipped to about ⅛ inch high for a fuzzy effect.

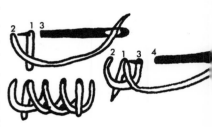

KNOT STITCHES

French Knot

This popular stitch may be used for flowers, borders, buttons, eyes, filling, etc. Bring needle through fabric at 1. Wrap yarn around needle (usually one wrap, but two or three wraps will work if you want a larger knot). Pull yarn snugly around needle and hold yarn in place with thumb as you insert needle back into fabric at point 2, which is right next to point 1. (Yarn does not have to be held snugly if you desire a large shaggy knot.)

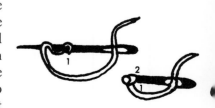

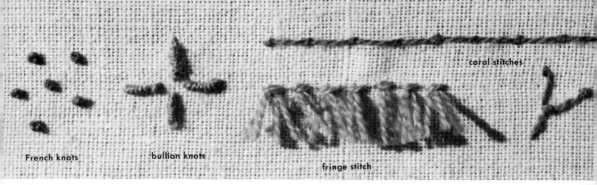

French knots   bullion knots   coral stitches   fringe stitch

Knot stitches

Bullion Knot

Often used for stems or grass, the bullion knot is usually made with a small-eyed needle that passes through the coils easily. Insert needle in fabric at 1 and out at 2 without pulling needle through. (The distance between 1 and 2 determines the size of the knot.) Wrap the yarn around the needle as many times as required to equal the space between 1 and 2. Hold the coiled yarn in place with your left thumb as you pull the needle through. Then insert the needle in point 1 and pull through, which tightens the stitch against the fabric.

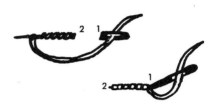

Coral Stitch

Working from right to left, pull needle through at 1. Insert needle in at 2 and out at 3 without pulling through. Then make a loop with needle passing *under* top of loop and *over* the bottom of the loop. Hold the yarn in place between points 1 and 2 and pull the yarn through. This makes a small slanting stitch that knots the yarn. Point 3 becomes the starting point for the next stitch. Keep knots evenly spaced.

Fringe Stitch

To make a fringed border, insert the needle in at 1 and out at 2, leaving a tail on top of the fabric. (The length of tail depends on how long you want the fringe to be.) Insert needle in at 3 and out at 1 keeping yarn *above* needle. Pull snugly to anchor stitch and cut yarn, leaving a tail the same length as the first tail. Continue making stitches until border is complete. Tails may be trimmed when finished.

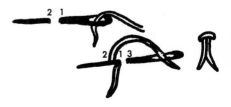

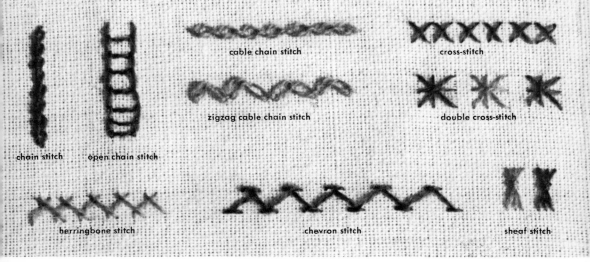

cable chain stitch

zigzag cable chain stitch

cross-stitch

double cross-stitch

chain stitch   open chain stitch

herringbone stitch   chevron stitch   sheaf stitch

Linked stitches

LINKED STITCHES

Chain Stitch

Useful for outlining, stems, and filling, the chain stitch is worked from bottom to top or right to left. Pull needle through at 1. Push needle in at 2 (right next to 1) and up at 3, making a loop of yarn *under* the needle. Pull through. Point 3 is now the starting point for the next stitch.

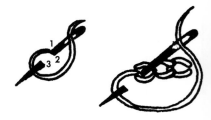

Open Chain Stitch

Working from top to bottom, bring needle through at 1. Push needle in at 2 and out at 3, making a loop *under* the needle. Pull through, leaving a loose loop, and push needle in at 4 and out at 5. Pull through, tightening the above loop. Keep stitches an equal distance apart. The last loop may be secured with a small stitch at each side.

Cable Chain Stitch

This stitch is worked like the chain stitch except that yarn is wrapped around the needle before inserting at 2. Pull needle through at 1 and wrap yarn once around needle before going in at 2 and out at 3. Make a loop *under* needle before pulling through. Point 3 is now the beginning of the next stitch.

Zigzag Cable Chain Stitch

Work this stitch exactly as you would the cable chain stitch except the needle is slanted at a right angle to the previous stitch between points 2 and 3.

Cross-stitch

An easy yet effective stitch, the cross-stitch is made by working a row of slanting stitches to form the first half of each cross. Work from right to left making stitches of equal size. When the row is complete, work back from left to right completing the other half of the cross.

Double Cross-stitch

Make a single cross-stitch, then work another cross-stitch over it diagonally. Keep stitches of equal length.

Herringbone Stitch

Working from left to right, bring needle through at 1. Make a small backstitch between points 2 and 3 on upper line. Make a small backstitch between points 4 and 5 on lower line. Continue until line is complete, aiming for evenly spaced stitches.

Chevron Stitch

Again working from right to left, bring needle through at 1, in at 2, and out at 3. Pull through. Make a straight stitch to the upper line going in at 4, then out at 5. Pull through. Then go in at 6 and out at 4, keeping yarn *above* needle. Return to bottom line going in at 7, out at 8, in at 9, out at 7, etc.

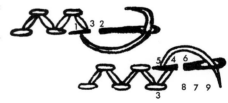

Sheaf Stitch

Also called the bundle stitch, the sheaf stitch is easily made by first completing three or four straight stitches. Then bring needle up beneath them at center and out to the left. Wrap the yarn around the straight stitches twice without piercing fabric. Push needle back through center.

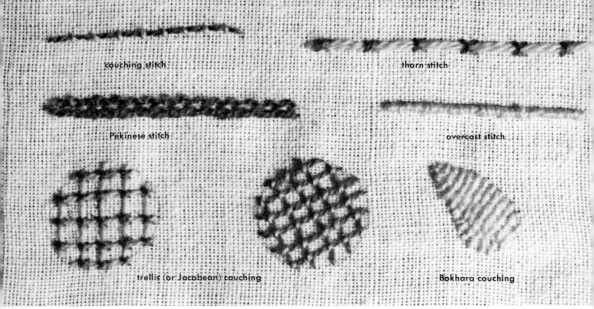

couching stitch

thorn stitch

Pekinese stitch

overcast stitch

trellis (or Jacobean) couching

Bokhara couching

Couching stitches

COUCHING STITCHES

Couching Stitch

Couching stitches use two threads, often of different colors. One thread is "laid" on the fabric and the other thread is "worked" over the laid thread. In the basic couching stitch, the first thread is pulled through the fabric then placed (or laid) in whatever direction you desire. The second thread is worked over the first thread by making small taut stitches at regular intervals. Thus, the working thread anchors the laid thread. When the desired length is completed, both threads should be pushed to the back of the fabric and secured.

Thorn Stitch

The thorn stitch is exactly like the couching stitch except that cross-stitches are used to anchor the first thread rather than single stitches.

Overcast Stitch

Useful for monogramming, heavy outlining, and stems, the overcast stitch is made exactly like the couching stitch except that the laid thread is completely covered by the working thread in small close satin stitches.

Pekinese Stitch

Work a line of backstitches. Then lace the
second thread (a contrasting color is effective)
through the backstitches without piercing the
fabric. Loops should be pulled slightly when
working to maintain an even appearance.

Trellis (or Jacobean) Couching

A very attractive filling stitch, trellis couching
is made by first laying long, evenly spaced
stitches horizontally and vertically (or diagonally). Then tie down the crossed threads at
all intersecting points with a small slanting
stitch or a cross-stitch.

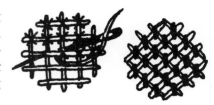

Bokhara Couching

This ornamental stitch is useful for filling in
leaves and flower petals. It is worked exactly
like the Romanian stitch except that the laid
stitch is tied several times at regular intervals
to form a pattern instead of being tied only
once in the center. The laid thread should be
slightly loose and the tying stitches should be
pulled tight. You may use the same thread for
all stitches.

WEAVING STITCHES

Needle Weaving

Similar to sock darning, weaving stitches are
made by first placing long vertical straight
stitches from top to bottom. Then (often
using a contrasting color) make horizontal
straight stitches, weaving the yarn in and out
of the vertical threads. Horizontal threads will
alternately go under or over the vertical
threads. The needle only pierces the fabric
when pulling through to start the horizontal
line and when ending the line. Do not pierce
fabric while weaving. (It is easier to use a
blunt tapestry needle or the eye end of a crewel
needle to avoid piercing fabric while weaving.)

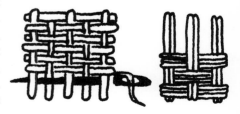

You may vary needle weaving by using several satin stitches for the vertical base instead

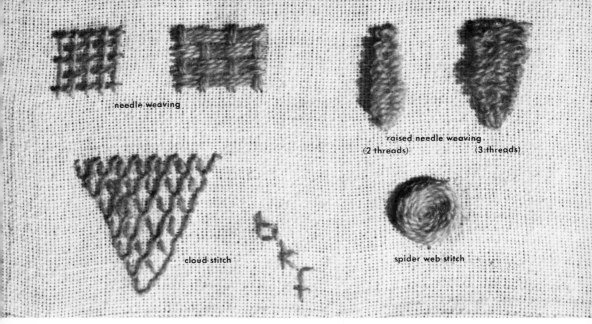

needle weaving

raised needle weaving
(2 threads)   (3 threads)

cloud stitch   spider web stitch

Woven stitches

of one straight stitch and by making several horizontal stitches in the same weave before alternating the over-under pattern.

Raised Needle Weaving

Raised needle weaving differs from normal needle weaving in that the horizontal thread is completely woven around the vertical threads. It does not go through the fabric except to start and finish.

Using a two-bar weave, make a vertical base by coming out at 1, in at 2, out again at 1, in again at 2. Come out at 1 once more to begin the horizontal weaving. Without piercing the fabric, bring needle over the left-hand bar, through the center, and under the right-hand bar. Pull through. Repeat the process in reverse by going over the right-hand bar, through the center, and under the left-hand bar. Pull through. Continue the over and under motions until the vertical bars are covered. Maintain even tension so the line will be smooth.

This stitch may be varied by using three bars as a vertical base. Come out at 1, in at 2, out at 1, in at 3, out at 1, in at 4. Begin weaving at point 1 without piercing fabric. The first row will go over, under, over; the next row will go under, over, under. Continue alternating the horizontal weave until the vertical bars are covered. Pull through after each woven row to keep yarn even and taut.

Cloud Stitch

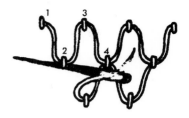

An effective filling stitch for many shapes, the cloud stitch is made by first placing several rows of small straight stitches that alternate from row to row. Then, using another thread (perhaps a different color), come through at 1 and weave yarn under small stitches zigzagging from one row of stitches to the other. For example, weave through point 2, then point 3, point 4, etc. Continue until shape is filled.

Spider Web Stitch

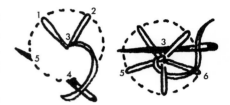

There are several ways to make a spider web stitch but the one shown is perhaps the easiest. Make a fly stitch by coming out at 1, in at 2, out at 3, and in at 4. Then add two straight stitches (one on each side of the fly stitch tail) by coming out at 5 and in at 3, out at 6, and in at 3. This divides the circle into five evenly spaced sections and forms the foundation of your web. Bring the yarn back out next to the center (3) and begin weaving over and under the web until the circle is filled.

FIVE

STEP FOUR... PUT IT ALL TOGETHER

After gathering materials, selecting a design, and choosing the stitches, you are now ready to begin the most exciting step of all: putting it all together. Now you can actually start to create a colorful stitchery picture.

Few directions are needed during the actual stitching process. Just enjoy the relaxation and creativity. However, the following step by step directions will ensure successful results.

TEN TIPS TO SUCCESS

1. Cut fabric at least 2 inches bigger than the size of the completed project. To prevent frayed edges, you may machine stitch the edges or cover them with masking tape. Place fabric on stretcher or in hoop. Tiny designs or raised stitches are sometimes easier to stitch when the fabric is held taut by hand.

2. Decide what to stitch first. Usually you may begin anywhere you want. Some stitchers prefer to fill in large designs first. Some like to complete the flat stitches first. Others like to start at the top and work their way down. And still others stitch one color first, then continue to the next color.

However, if one design is on top of another design, the bottom design is stitched first. For example, you would stitch a ladybug's body first, then add the outline and spots. If you were stitching a strawberry, you would stitch the fruit itself first, then add the seeds and cap.

3. Select the yarn for the design you will stitch first. Cut the yarn in 2-foot lengths, or about arm's length. This size enables you to stitch without the yarn becoming tangled or frayed. (If you will be doing a great deal of stitchery, you may wish to precut all your yarn and wrap it around cardboard or hang it on cup hooks on a board. Then you can simply reach for the yarn as you need it.) Also, if you will be using only one or two strands of a 3-ply yarn, now is the time to separate the strands.

4. Thread the needle by moistening the end and inserting. Sometimes the slim eye of a crewel needle makes threading difficult. To overcome this, you may pinch the yarn around the needle, then insert (as pictured). Or, easier yet, cut a tiny strip of paper (about ¼ inch wide and 2 inches long), fold, insert yarn in fold, then push through the needle's eye.

5. In normal sewing, knots are used to secure the end of the thread. However, knots may cause lumps or become undone when using yarn. Knots may be used with stitches that are lumpy enough to hide the knot, such as French knots or the loose loop stitch. And knots may be used when the completed project will not be flattened, such as pillows. But, if the completed project will be framed flat against a cardboard backing, you may wish to avoid knots by leaving a 1-inch tail in back and stitching over it; by making a few small running stitches along the line to be embroidered, then one backstitch; or by sliding the needle through a few stitches already on the back of the fabric.

6. Fill in the design by "stabbing" the fabric with the needle. That is, stab the needle straight up and down through the fabric, pulling the yarn through each time (with the exception of looped or linked stitches where the needle must come out ahead to catch the yarn). Place the needle where the completed stitch will cover the design line entirely. Otherwise lines will show through when you are finished.

Be guided by the weave of the fabric whenever you want stitches to be even vertically and horizontally. For example, when doing a running stitch, make sure the needle always goes in and out along the same thread line of the fabric. Even double cross-stitches will turn out perfectly by always placing the needle on the same horizontal and vertical thread. In fact, by following the weave of the fabric, you will not need patterns for borders, stems, fringe, or any other design that adheres to the weave.

7. Put your other hand to work. As one hand pushes and pulls the needle, use your other hand to guide the yarn and keep it out of the needle's way. Many stitches require that the yarn be kept above or below the needle. This is the job of the left thumb.

Try to stitch with even tension. In other words, do not pull the yarn too tightly or you will pucker the fabric. And do not forget to pull the yarn snugly against the fabric or you will have a sloppy looking stitch.

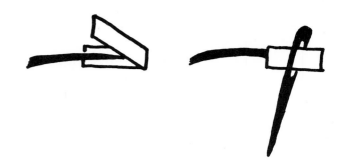

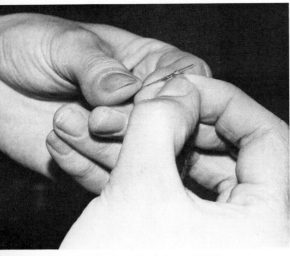

Another simple threading technique is to first insert yarn in a narrow strip of folded paper, then push through the needle's eye.

A simple way to thread a needle with yarn is to first squeeze the yarn tightly around the needle.

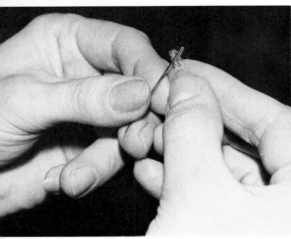

Then force the eye of the needle onto the fold of the yarn and pull the remainder through.

8. If you are dissatisfied with a stitch, do not care for a particular color selection, or want to use more or less strands than originally intended, that is no problem. Simply pull out the unwanted yarn and start over.

9. If the yarn becomes tangled as you stitch, dangle the needle to unwind.

10. When you have completed a color or design and wish to end the thread, again it may be necessary to avoid knots. If so, push the needle to the reverse side and weave it in and out of the last few stitches. Use scissors to cut the thread close to the fabric.

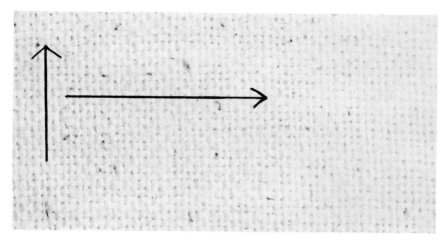

Follow the weave of the fabric for perfectly placed stitches.

Use your left thumb to guide the yarn, keeping it above or below the needle as the stitch requires.

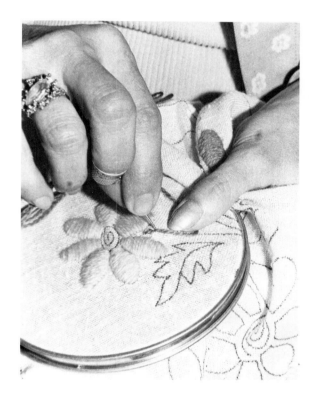

It is usually best to end a thread when a particular design is finished rather than skip to another part of the design with the same thread. The trailing yarn may show through or be lumpy when finished.

As you stitch, you will begin to notice that each stitch has a rhythm, such as one, two, three, one, two, three. This rhythm not only makes stitchery a very relaxing hobby, but it is a clue that you are stitching correctly. If, after several projects, you fail to notice a rhythm, it is probably because you are worrying too much about your work. The answer is to relax.

CLEANING AND BLOCKING

Hopefully your stitchery has remained clean during the stitching process. To ensure cleanliness, wash hands before stitching and always store unfinished projects in a cupboard, plastic bag, or workbasket where they will be protected from dust and soil. While stitching, place your project out of the way of coffee spills and cigarette ashes. In case "first aid" is needed, here is what to do.

Clean soiled fabric with dry cleaning fluid or by hand washing in cold water with a gentle detergent. (Washable fabrics and yarns may be machine washed on gentle cycle with warm water.) Rinse thoroughly but do not wring. Instead, let drip for a few minutes, then tack to a wooden frame or stretcher to block fabric to original size. Or, use pushpins to hold fabric to cardboard covered by a towel. Thus, the tacks or pins hold the fabric where you want it as it dries. (Or, play it safe by taking your stitchery to a competent dry cleaner for cleaning and blocking.)

Often fabric isn't soiled but merely has "ghosts" of the yarn clinging to it. Remove these by dabbing with masking tape wrapped around your hand.

Protect your stitchery from further soiling by spraying it with a spray-on fabric protector, available in the detergent section of grocery stores. Read directions on the can carefully and check for colorfastness before using.

Blocking fabric (stretching it back to its original shape) is recommended when the fabric has been pulled or puckered out of shape while stitching. You will probably need to block the fabric unless you used a stretcher or hoop larger than your design.

Blocking is easily done by tacking the fabric to a stretcher, wooden frame, heavy cardboard, etc. Stretch the fabric into shape and keep it that way by placing pushpins, tacks, or staples around the edges of the fabric about an inch apart. By the next morning, the fabric should be ready to frame. (If stitchery is badly puckered, you may need to dampen it before stretching back into normal shape.)

With smaller designs, you may be able to smooth the fabric by ironing it on the reverse side. Use gentle pressure where the iron touches the stitches or it will flatten them.

FRAMING STITCHERY PICTURES

Selecting a frame for your stitchery picture is as crucial as selecting a color or a stitch. After all, the frame will become part of the picture too!

The least expensive frames will be found at the dime store. Select the size that best suits the size of the design, such as 4" x 5", 11" x 14", and so forth. If the frame is prefinished, select a natural wood color, gold metal color, or color that coordinates with your design. If the frame is unfinished wood, stain or paint it in a color that enhances the design.

For example, if the design is extremely colorful, a natural wood stain may show it off to best advantage. If you wish to stress the dominant color in a design, such as turquoise, then paint the frame turquoise to bring out the color in the design. (Do not use the glass that comes with some frames because it will flatten the stitches.)

Often the most exciting frames are found in frame shops that cater to artists. (Look under "Picture Frames" in the Yellow Pages.) These shops can also custom-make frames to suit your particular design.

Or, you can make your own frame out of driftwood or old barn wood or even inexpensive laths. Homemade frames are particularly effective on seascapes, landscapes, Old West, and antique designs.

Another idea is to use no frame at all. Just leave the stitchery in an appropriately sized hoop or on the stretcher and hang it stretcher and all! Or, hem the bottom and top of the stitchery fabric about 1 inch wide. Then insert a round dowel through each hem, attach rope or a leather thong to the ends of the top dowel, and hang.

Whenever a regular frame is used, the fabric will need to be held taut so that it won't sag. You may tack or staple the fabric to the inside frame. Or, better yet, cut a piece of cardboard to fit inside the frame. The fabric may be pulled to the back of the cardboard and stapled, glued, or taped to the cardboard to hold it taut.

Sometimes it is possible to cut corners by gluing the fabric directly on the cardboard with white craft glue. After the glue is evenly distributed with a brush or finger, place the fabric on the cardboard, stretching it into place where needed. Make sure the fabric weave remains vertical and horizontal. Insert cardboard with fabric forward into the frame and hang. This shortcut is dandy for small projects, such as Christmas ornaments and stationary designs, but it will emphasize any lumps, knots, or trailing yarn on the back. Thus, it is not recommended for large designs or serious projects.

THE STITCHER IS ALWAYS RIGHT

That's it! In four simple steps, you have created a stitchery picture that can perk up any room with its warmth and beauty. Following these same four steps, you can now stitch any design or project that catches your fancy.

And, to catch your fancy, the remainder of this book is filled with popular patterns, original designs, and practical projects. Although most projects give step by step instructions for colors and stitches, don't be afraid to substitute your own selections. Your own ideas give your work a stamp of individuality! (Do stitch your name or initials and date on your work so friends will know whose individuality it shows.)

A final word to beginning stitchers. The biggest bugaboo to overcome is worrying about whether or not you are doing the "right" thing. The

By following the four easy steps given in the preceding chapters, this adorable mushroom design was completed from start to finish in one evening. (Gather materials, create or copy a design, select the stitches, and put it all together.) Design and stitchery by B. Kay Fraser.

wonderful fact about stitchery is that there are no rights or wrongs. If you like a color scheme, use it. If a strange design appeals to you, stitch it. If you find an unusual fabric or yarn, try it. The greatest art in the world has been produced by people who create to please themselves. So, if we must give stitchery a rule, it should be: The stitcher is always right!

Stitchery pictures are easily mounted in a picture frame with the help of cardboard and glue or masking tape.

SIX

PRACTICE WITH POPULAR PATTERNS

By following the four basic steps given in the preceding chapters, you can now stitch any design imaginable. To demonstrate just how easy these four steps can be (gather materials, create or copy a design, select the stitches, and put it all together), this chapter features stitchery projects that were completed by following these steps. Because these projects are so beautiful, you may wish to copy them (see Chapter 3) or use them as examples to inspire your original ideas.

CREATING FROM CARDS

An excellent source of contemporary art is today's greeting cards. The best selection will be found in card and gift shops, drugstores, and department stores.

Most card designs will need to be enlarged, and many designs can easily be altered into your own creation. For example, on the little girl shown, the stitcher was inspired by a card. But the flowers are original, the dress design changed, and the colors are the stitcher's selection.
1. Materials: White synthetic linen and Persian yarn.
2. Design: Inspired from a greeting card and combined with stitcher's own designs.

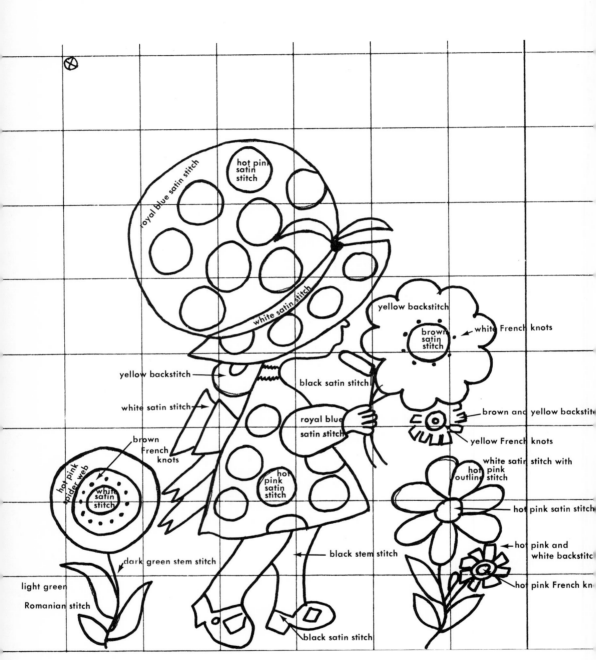

Pattern for "Polka-dot Girl with Flowers."

3. Stitches: As shown on diagram. Stitches were selected for their variety and ability to convey texture. Satin stitches use two strands of yarn; all other stitches use one. Clothing is outlined in stem stitch.

"Polka-dot Girl with Flowers" by Skip McGarvery.

4. Putting it together: Begin with the little girl, then stitch the flowers. Because the girl is the main design, the flowers can be rearranged or colors changed to enhance her. The design was tacked to a stretcher rather than being framed.

SHARING IDEAS WITH FRIENDS

Many stitchers gain ideas from the work of other stitchers. In fact, many stitchers are organized into clubs and groups simply to share ideas and learn from one another.

The design shown, "Don't Bug Me Baby," was completed by Lorrie Trano and displayed to fellow stitchers at The Eugene Stitcher's Guild in Eugene, Oregon.

1. Materials: Off-white hopsacking fabric and mohair yarn.
2. Design: Composed by Lorrie Trano.
3. Stitches: As shown on diagram. Bugs are filled in with tightly spaced looped seeding stitches. Make normal seeding stitch but do not pull yarn completely through. Leave yarn in about a ⅛-inch loop instead of pulling taut.
4. Putting it together: Stitch bugs' bodies first, then add arms, legs, and facial features. The design was unframed and tacked to a stretcher for hanging.

Pattern for "Don't Bug Me Baby."

"Don't Bug Me Baby" by Lorrie Trano.

CONFIDENCE FROM KITS

As mentioned earlier, stitchery kits provide an excellent means for beginning stitchers to build up confidence. In fact, many talented original stitchers began by completing a kit. And many experienced stitchers still use kits occasionally because they are so handy and feature beautiful designs.

However, kits do vary in quality and ingredients. The best kits are found in quality department stores, art needlework stores, and through craft catalogs. (All kit manufacturers represented in this book feature excellent quality fabric and yarns and are highly recommended.)

You have already learned in previous chapters how to compose your own stitchery kit. These techniques will be helpful when stitching a manufactured kit. You may wish to change a color, design, or stitch. Or, you may wonder how to clean, block, or frame the kit. Or perhaps a stitch diagram may be unclear to you. So this book will be a helpful reference as you stitch.

To illustrate how kits work, Sunset Designs has allowed us to use their designs as an example. The patterns and instructions for "Fuzzy Teddy" (His) and "Fuzzy Teddy" (Hers) are exactly as they appear in the kits. (Kit instructions, however, also include stitch diagrams and

"Fuzzy Teddy" designs are manufactured in kit form by Sunset Designs and are available in art needlework and department stores.

helpful hints that have been discussed earlier in the book.) Kits contain all fabric, yarn, and needles needed to complete the design.

1. Materials: Cream-colored linen weave fabric and 3-ply Persian yarn (only one strand is used unless otherwise noted).
2. Design: By Charlene Gerrish for Sunset Designs, 1990 Olivera Road, Concord, California 94520.
3. Stitches: As shown. Ms. Gerrish selected a variety of stitches that give realistic texture and bright color. Colors are keyed by number on the pattern, and the stitching sequence is given in the instructions.
4. Putting it together: Follow the stitching sequence given in instructions. When completed, the designs were mounted with cardboard backing in walnut-stained wood frames also available from Sunset Designs.

Pattern for "Fuzzy Teddy" (His) by Charlene Gerrish for Sunset Designs.

COLOR GUIDE

*1. Brown
*2. Red
*3. Dark Blue

*4. Light Blue
*5. Light Yellow
6. Dark Yellow/Gold
7. Black

Instructions for "Fuzzy Teddy" (His)

A. Backstitch all heavy lines (indicated on drawing), in color 1. Use very small stitches for features. Backstitch around all areas on train, 1. Place four French knots for wheels of train, using double-ply, 1. Place one French knot in center of large train wheel, using single-ply, 1.

B. Satin stitch areas of train marked 2. Satin stitch emblem on hat, 2.

* Three-ply yarn. Please separate to 1-ply unless otherwise noted.

C. Satin stitch bill of cap, 3. Stem stitch lines on cap, 3. Stem stitch shirt outline at shoulder and sleeve, 3. Stem stitch lines on shirt, 3. Use two rows of stem stitch for bottom line, 3.

D. Use parallel rows of stem stitch to fill bands on shirt, 4. Satin stitch area of train marked 4. Outline circles of smoke in backstitch, 4.

E. Satin stitch muzzle, slipping needle under mouth lines, 5. Satin stitch ear areas marked 5. Satin stitch paw pads, 5.

F. Satin stitch pupils of bear's eyes, 7. Satin stitch roof and cow catcher on train, 7.

G. Work bear's body, head and ears in looped stem, 6. Broken lines in these areas indicate the number of rows of stitches. Work outer rows of looped stem $\frac{1}{16}$ inch in from edge. Make stitches about $\frac{1}{8}$ inch long and $\frac{1}{4}$ inch high. In areas where only one row of looped stem is needed, make stitches very small.

H. Clip looped stem to about $\frac{1}{8}$ inch high. Clip very close to fabric near edges and around features so that outline shows. Any areas that need to be filled in after clipping can be filled by knotting yarn, pulling up through fabric from back, and clipping to desired length. Masking tape may be used to pick up fuzz from background fabric.

I. Place one French knot on front of train, 6, indicated on drawing by dot.

J. Make one long straight stitch from dot on bear's paw to French knot on front of train, 7. Leave the stitch loose. Make a French knot, using double-ply, for bear's nose, 7. (Refer to drawing or photograph for placement.)

Instructions for "Fuzzy Teddy" (Hers)

A. Satin stitch pupils of eyes using color 1. Place one French knot, using double strand, for nose, 1.

B. Backstitch with very small stitches around outline of eyes, 2. Backstitch mouth lines with very small stitches, 2. (Refer to drawing and photograph for exact expression.)

C. Backstitch outline of bear, basket, and basket handle as indicated by heavy lines on drawing, 2.

D. Place two long straight stitches on each vertical basket line, 2. Weave with color 4. (Refer to weaving stitch diagram.)

E. Fill centers of butterfly wings with satin stitches, 4. Fill basket handle with two rows of stem stitch, 4.

F. Satin stitch ear areas marked 5. Satin stitch three paw pads, 5. Satin stitch face area marked 5, slipping needle under lines of mouth.

G. Using color 6, make French knots on each of the flowers and flower centers, indicated on drawing by small open circles.

H. Place three French knots on knot cluster, lower left flower, indicated on drawing by filled-in dots, 7. Satin and straight stitch outer area of butterfly wings, 7.

I. Dress Skirt: On all lines of bear's skirt, including edges already outlined, use squared filling. Long straight stitches are *double strand*

Pattern for "Fuzzy Teddy" (Hers) by Charlene Gerrish for Sunset Designs.

COLOR GUIDE

1. Black
*2. Dark Brown
3. Light Brown
4. Yellow

*5. Flesh
6. Light Pink
7. Dark Pink
8. Green

color 6. Tack these down at intersections with color 7. (Refer to illustration for squared filling.)

J.   Satin stitch bear's bodice, 8. Straight stitch grass in lower right corner, 8. Straight stitch the two flower stems in basket and in the lower left corner, 8. Lazy daisy flower leaves, 8. (Leaves are filled in on drawing.)

K.   Lazy daisy flower petals, 7.

L.   Work bear's ears, face, and paws in looped stem stitch, 3. Broken lines in these areas indicate the number of rows of stitches. Work outer rows of looped stem $\frac{1}{16}$ inch in from edge. Make stitches about $\frac{1}{8}$ inch long and $\frac{1}{4}$ inch high. In areas where only one row of looped stem is needed, make stitches very small.

* Three-ply yarn. Please separate to 1-ply unless otherwise noted.

M. Clip looped stem to about ⅛ inch high. Clip very close to fabric near edges and around features so that outline shows. Any areas that need to be filled in after clipping can be filled by knotting yarn, pulling up through material from back, and clipping to desired length. Masking tape may be used to pick up fuzz from background fabric.

N. There are three flower stems and one grass blade shadowed with color 2, indicated on drawing by broken lines. Straight stitch these broken lines, 2. Place one long straight stitch for body of butterfly, 2. (Refer to drawing or photograph for placement.)

O. Place two long straight stitches for stem of flower in bear's hand, 8. (Refer to drawing and photograph for placement.) Place French knot in center of flower in bear's hand, 8.

P. Cover the petals of flower on bear's face again with lazy daisy stitches, color 7, so that it will show over fuzzy area.

NEWSPAPER STITCHERY

One of the most exciting and easy-to-find sources of stitchery designs is the newspaper. Grocery ads are full of fruits and vegetables that are easily copied. Florist shops often advertise with floral designs. Real estate developments sometimes feature sketches of trees and lakes. And don't overlook the sports section for photos of wildlife and fish.

An example of newspaper stitchery is this vegetable ecology box that was copied from grocery advertisements. See what you can create from last night's paper!

1. Materials: White linen weave fabric and 3-ply Persian yarn.

2. Design: Traced from a newspaper grocery advertisement . . . no enlarging was necessary.

3. Stitches: Stitches and colors were selected to give the vegetables as realistic an appearance as possible. Stitches, colors, and strands are shown on the pattern.

4. Putting it together: The ecology box was purchased unassembled and stained in walnut (available in craft stores, hobby stores, and through craft catalogs). Measure the size of each box, then select a design that will fit. Each vegetable was completed individually, then mounted on cardboard with masking tape for insertion in box. Because the box was deep, an extra layer of cardboard was placed behind the design to make it stand out more.

Pattern for "Vegetable Ecology Box."

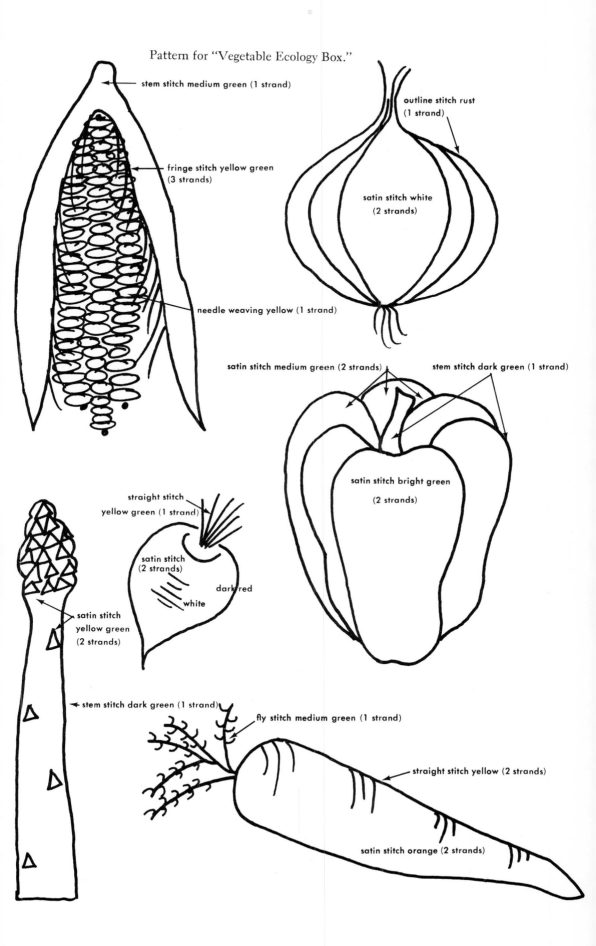

stem stitch medium green (1 strand)

outline stitch rust
(1 strand)

satin stitch white
(2 strands)

fringe stitch yellow green
(3 strands)

needle weaving yellow (1 strand)

satin stitch medium green (2 strands)

stem stitch dark green (1 strand)

satin stitch bright green

(2 strands)

straight stitch
yellow green (1 strand)

satin stitch
(2 strands)

dark red

white

satin stitch
yellow green
(2 strands)

stem stitch dark green (1 strand)

fly stitch medium green (1 strand)

straight stitch yellow (2 strands)

satin stitch orange (2 strands)

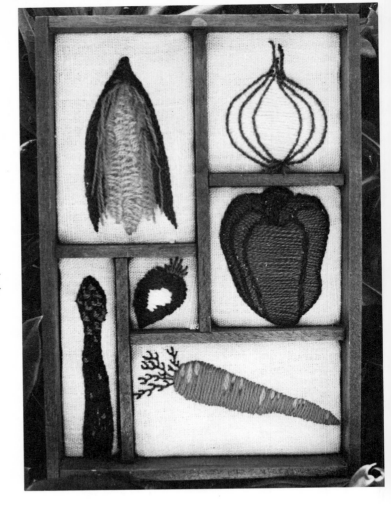

"Vegetable Ecology Box" by B. Kay Fraser.

FUN WITH FOLK ART

Another source of inspiration for stitchery designs is folk art—art created by our early settlers and native Indians. White settlers brought favorite designs to Canada and the United States from Europe. Many of these designs are enjoying a rebirth in popularity, particularly through tole painting. Any tole painting design is easily adapted to stitchery. And don't overlook the folk art of our continent's original inhabitants—the Indians. Indian designs are not only colorful and stunning, but each design has a story behind it. Browse through museums and libraries for the best selection of Indian designs.

An example of yesteryear's Indian art is the thunderbird, one of the most widely known folk designs, and it appears in various forms among tribes throughout the North American continent. (The thunderbird was usually believed to be an enormous super-being who lived in human form on the highest mountain peaks. But when he searched for food, he was transformed into a gigantic bird so large that his body hid the sun and darkened the sky. And the beating of his huge wings caused thunder.)

1. Materials: Turquoise synthetic linen weave fabric and 3-ply Persian yarn.
2. Design: Form of thunderbird adapted to stitchery by B. Kay Fraser.
3. Stitches: Straight stitches with one strand of black yarn were used to fill the thunderbird's body. Double strands of white, red, and tur-

Pattern for "Thunderbird."

"Thunderbird" by B. Kay Fraser.

quoise were used on the stomach, tongue, teeth, eye, and head feathers in satin stitch. Accent designs on wings are red stem stitch (one strand); yellow backstitch (one strand); and satin stitches (two strands) in white, turquoise, and bright green. When all designs were stitched, the bird's body was outlined in black stem stitch (one strand) to give a more finished appearance to straight stitches.

4. Putting it together: Because the thunderbird was enlarged to about 18 by 24 inches, it required many hours to complete. To prevent monotony, the stitcher alternated stitches and colors frequently. When finished, the design was framed in a homemade wooden frame made of laths and painted black.

IMITATING MOTHER NATURE

Perhaps the best source of stitchery designs is Mother Nature herself. The grace and color of natural scenery that surrounds us is the best inspiration of all.

An easy way to imitate Mother Nature is to sketch a flower or tree with pencil and paper as you look at it. Decide which stitches and colors would best duplicate Mother Nature's design. Or, take a photograph of the flower or foliage and have it enlarged to the desired size. Then trace the photograph to use as a pattern.

An excellent example of reproducing Mother Nature in stitchery is the Queen Anne's lace shown. Even dew is added to flower petals by the clever addition of clear beads. An exclusive design of LeeWards Creative Crafts, Inc., this design is available in kit form at LeeWards stores or through their catalog (address below). The kit contains all materials needed, including instructions, fabric, yarn, needle, beads, frame, and paint.

1. Materials: Avocado green Serrano fabric and crewel yarn.
2. Design: Queen Anne's Lace Picture Kit by LeeWards Creative Crafts, Inc., 1200 St. Charles Road, Elgin, Illinois 60120.
3. Stitches: Only four simple stitches using one strand of yarn are required to realistically imitate these flowers. LeeWards instructions refer to colors by letters and stitches by numbers. This is the code used to complete the design shown:

stitches	colors
No. 3 = straight stitch	A = white
No. 2 = satin stitch	B = dark golden brown
No. 15 = lazy daisy stitch	C = medium rust
No. 16 = French knots	D = light rust
	E = light burnt olive
	G = bright olive
	H = light olive green
	J = dark sage green
	L = shaded yellow (embroidery thread)

Pattern for "Queen Anne's Lace" by LeeWards Creative Crafts, Inc. ➤

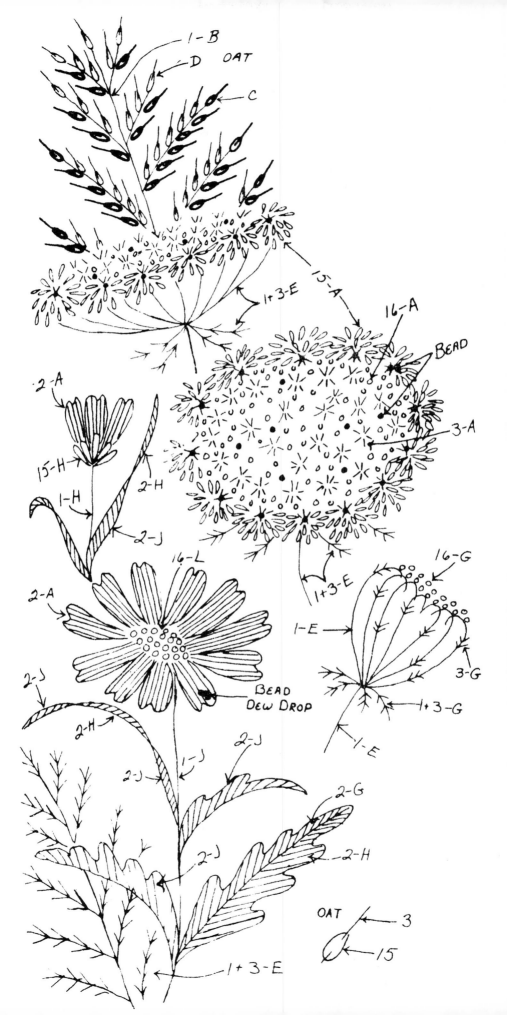

4. Putting it together: LeeWards suggests that you complete the design in the following four steps. (Hint—separate yarn into different color piles and keep colored picture on kit box.)

Step 1. No. 16 French knots done with color A only wrapped once around needle.

Step 2. Daisy Centers. Using shaded color L, cut a piece long enough to have darkest shade at one end and lightest at another. Start with bottom row of French knots 16–L and darkest shade, work back and forth so that thread will get lighter as it reaches the top row of knots. Use the full six strands of color L.

Step 3. Beads. Place beads as indicated by small black dots. Beads in center of Queen Anne's lace are placed at random. Sew all beads on by using one strand of color L.

Step 4. Daisy Dewdrops. Choose one lower petal of a daisy and use three beads strung togther and sew to petal, making them slightly humped.

"Queen Anne's Lace" Picture Kit by LeeWards Creative Crafts, Inc. Stitched by Ila Mae Robinson.

SEVEN

CREATE YOUR OWN DESIGNS

Although stitching popular patterns is an exciting and fulfilling craft, don't overlook the self-satisfaction of creating your own designs. You may be surprised to learn that original stitchery is often just as easy as stitching from copied designs.

To create your own design, simply draw the design on paper first, then transfer it to fabric (as explained in Chapter 3). Or, you may simply start stitching, using yarn on fabric as an artist would use oils on canvas.

The most difficult part of creating your own design is convincing yourself you can do it! To help you get started, this chapter offers techniques and examples of original stitchery. The examples shown were created by a variety of persons, ranging from beginners to professional stitchery designers.

START WITH A SAMPLER

Before creating an original design, it will be helpful to have a working knowledge of a variety of stitches. So, if you have not yet tried all the stitches shown in Chapter 4, a sampler would be an excellent first original project. (You may also expand your stitch selection by referring

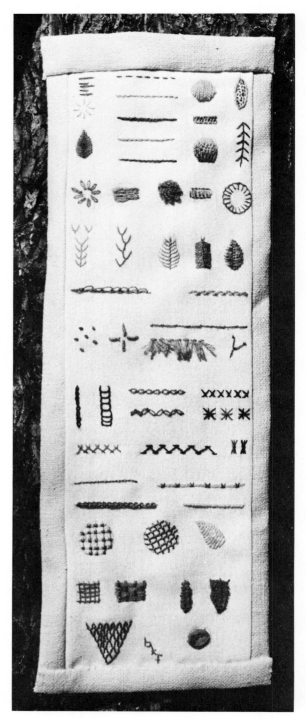

Original stitchery begins with a working knowledge of many stitches. The above sampler features the 45 stitches explained in Chapter 4. By B. Kay Fraser.

to embroidery stitch books available at the library, bookstore, or art needlework store.)

To make a sampler, select a fabric that has a distinct weave, such as linen or hopsacking. The weave will help you place your stitches more accurately. Use only one strand of yarn so you can see the finished effect of each stitch more clearly. By using a variety of yarn colors on white fabric, your sampler will also become a handy color guide for future projects.

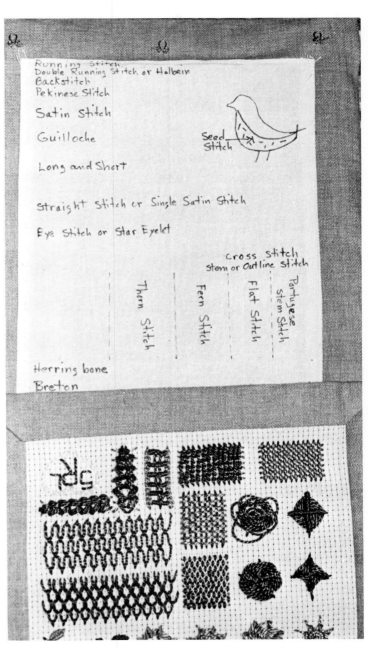

Running Stitch
Double Running Stitch or Holbein
Backstitch
Pekinese Stitch

Satin Stitch

Guilloche

Long and Short

Straight Stitch or Single Satin Stitch

Eye Stitch or Star Eyelet

Seed Stitch

Cross Stitch
Stem or Outline Stitch

Thorn Stitch

Fern Stitch

Flat Stitch

Portugese Stem Stitch

Herring bone
Breton

The names of each stitch on the back of a sampler become a useful guide. By Shirley Richards.

Add designs such as birds or flowers to a sampler for increased eye appeal. By Shirley Richards.

A sampler of linked stitches becomes more colorful with the addition of appliquéd fish. By Shirley Richards.

You may place your stitches at random on the sampler. Or, you may group stitch families together, such as flat stitches, looped stitches, etc. If space is a factor (say, you want the sampler to be 8 inches wide and 24 inches long), then you may use a ruler to measure how much space you can allow each stitch. Use a pencil to mark the distance in the fabric's margin. This will guide you as you stitch.

Because a sampler is such an excellent stitch reference, you should try to complete each stitch as accurately as possible. Remove unsatisfactory stitches and start over. It will be helpful to write the name of each stitch on the back of the fabric.

You may wish to enhance your sampler with designs as well as stitches. For example, you can stitch flowers or birds on the sampler. Or, you can add appliqué fish or fruit. Still another idea is to make a sampler by filling in a large design, such as a turtle's back or snail's shell.

When completed, your sampler can be framed with cloth or wood and displayed with pride ... because samplers are pretty as well as practical.

Using a variety of stitches on a large design is another way to create a sampler.
By Mary Ellen Harris.

Even a minisampler of stitches you have never tried is good practice. By Gayle
Decker.

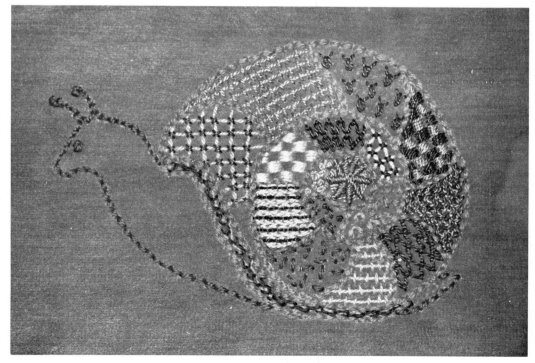

THREE "YOU CAN DO IT" TECHNIQUES

As mentioned earlier, the most difficult part of original designing is convincing yourself you can do it. So, to convince yourself how easily a design can be created, try one or more of the following techniques.

1. Select one stitch and compose a shape using only that stitch. For example, the "Mousetracks" design originated when the stitcher started making French knots. The "Sunset Hill" design resulted when the stitcher appliquéd black felt on orange fabric and used backstitches only to create the shapes of trees at sunset as seen from her window. The "Weaving in Hoops" design was made by using spider web weaving stitches in various size embroidery hoops. And the owl design emerged from rows and rows of chain stitching. See what you can do with only one stitch.

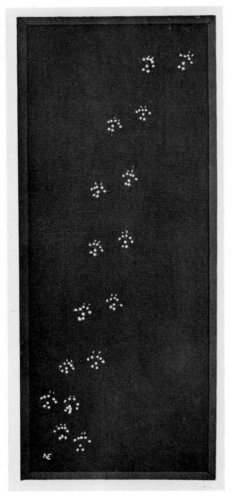

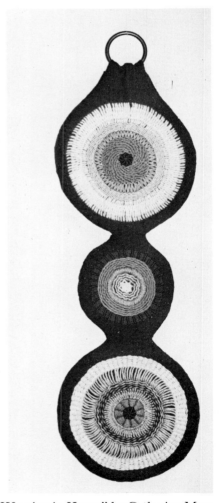

"Mousetracks" by Norma J. Evans.   "Weaving in Hoops" by Catherine Mace.

"Sunset Hill" by Dolly Chambers.

"Chain Stitch Owl" by Gayle Decker.

2. Cut a design with scissors and paper and use the paper's shape as an original pattern. Fold a piece of paper in half, fold in half again, and fold that in half. Then cut shapes with scissors (as children do to make snowflakes). Unfold the paper, and use it as the basis of your design, as shown.

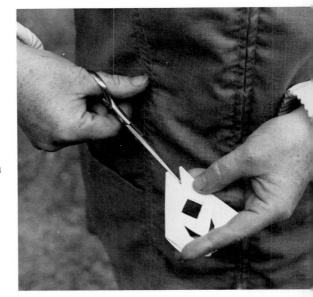

Cut designs in folded paper as a child would cut a snowflake.

The unfolded paper can now be used as a pattern.

"Snowflake Pillow" by Dolly Chambers.

3. Start stitching a favorite stitch on the bottom or in the middle of a piece of fabric and see what it suggests. Then complete the design to complement the suggested shape. As an example, the "Fairyland Mushroom" could have resulted when the stitcher created cloud stitch filling, which looks like a mushroom cap. Another example is the wheat design. A couching stitch dotted with French knots resembles a grain of wheat, so the stitcher continued duplicating the stitches until a wheat field emerged.

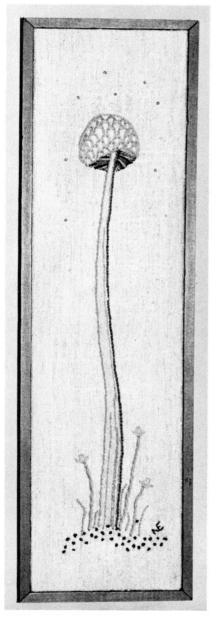

"Wheat Field" by Lois M. Smith.

"Fairyland Mushroom" by Norma J. Evans.

Create distance by making background objects smaller in proportion to objects in the foreground. "Pigeons' Paradise" by Lorrie Trano.

SHAPES, TEXTURES, COLORS

The most successful stitchery designs are those that re-create nature's shapes, textures, and colors. The best guide to design is the world around you. Notice the graceful shape of birds in flight. Feel the texture of leaves, bark, and flower petals. Observe the beauty of natural color schemes—sunsets, gardens, lakeshores, snowfalls.

The trick is to create this beauty in stitchery. Stitchery offers unique tools for re-creation. You can place your needle anywhere on fabric to stitch a desired shape. You can select a variety of stitches to duplicate natural texture. And a wide choice of yarn and fabric color makes any color scheme possible.

By trying to match shapes, stitches, and colors to nature's own, your stitchery will be elevated from average to professional quality. Let us take a closer look at each of these three points to help you hone your observation of natural design.

Shapes are perhaps the easiest to duplicate. An orange is round, a box is square, and so forth. The difficulty arises when things are perceived

Observe nature's shapes to create stitchery shapes. "Mallard Duck" by Lorrie Trano.

from a distance. For example, in a bouquet or cluster of grapes, the flowers or fruit that is farthest from you will appear smaller and darker. Thus, when you stitch, create smaller designs and use darker colors for objects that are farther away. By varying proportions, you create depth and dimension.

The same principle holds true in landscapes. Notice in "Pigeons' Paradise" that the main field narrows in back to create distance and that the barn in back is much smaller than the house.

Texture is created in stitchery by the stitches you select. The ability of stitches to convey texture is what sets stitchery apart from other crafts. Thus, stitch choice in original stitchery is crucial. The right stitch gives texture, warmth, dimension, and realism.

Fortunately, stitch selection is easy if you have made a sampler. Choose the stitch that comes closest to reproducing the true texture of the design. For example, on the spice set shown, notice how the designer used the Y- (also called fly) stitch to re-create caraway leaves; a woven bar (or raised needle weaving) stitch to imitate cinnamon leaves; and different size fishbone stitches to duplicate clove and nutmeg leaves. (Even wooden beads were covered with yarn for a realistic nutmeg!)

Another delightful, more advanced example of stitch selection is the planters shown. On the "Asparagus Fern," the designer not only made excellent use of needle weaving to create a basket and the fern stitch for background foliage, but she adapted macramé techniques to stitchery to create new stitches for cords and fern. With a little thought and willingness to experiment, you too can create unusual stitches.

Still another way to vary texture in stitchery is to use different types of yarn. For example, mohair yarn makes a more fluffy flower. Postal twine looks more like wood when stitching fences. And a metallic-like polyester thread creates "real" gold and silver objects.

All spice designs by Betty Miles for Sunset Designs. Available in kit form at art needlework and department stores.

"Prayer Plant" and "Asparagus Fern" designs by Charlene Gerrish for Sunset Designs. Available in kit form at art needlework and department stores.

Different types of yarn, such as mohair, can also vary the texture of your design. "Sunburst Flower" by Lorrie Trano.

Color selection is the third important factor in original stitchery. There are many opinions of what makes a good color scheme, but the easiest and most successful methods for stitchery are:

1. Choose colors that are pleasing to you. If you like bright reds and yellows, use them. If you prefer delicate pastels, use them. If you prefer dramatic black, use it. Colors reflect our moods and personalities, so it makes sense to use colors we like.

2. Choose colors to match a room. If you know where your stitchery will be displayed, then select colors that coordinate with that room's decor. For example, if the design will be hung in a room decorated in oranges and browns, then use these as main colors and perhaps greens and yellows for accents. Or, if the design will be hung in a blue room, use blues in the main design and green, lavender, and white as accents.

3. Choose colors to re-create nature. For example, select yellow for daffodils, green for grass, red for apples, and so forth. But do notice that Mother Nature usually has shadings and highlights. For example, an apple may appear red, but a closer look shows that (depending upon lighting conditions) the round part of the apple closest to you actually looks lighter—as if it has a yellow or white highlight. And the edges of the apple, which are farthest from you, may appear deep red or maroon. Thus, if you are seriously trying to duplicate

nature, remember to shade and highlight objects with slightly darker and slightly lighter colors.

Also, remember that objects farthest from you are darker and objects closer to you are lighter. For example, when stitching a group of leaves, the leaves farthest back would be dark green, middle leaves medium green, and closest leaves light or bright green.

Strangely enough, you will probably employ all three methods in color selection and end up using a color scheme Mother Nature already invented. Here is why. Colors that please you are probably colors you enjoy in nature such as refreshing forest greens and cheerful sun yellows. Colors that match your room decor are usually colors found outdoors, such as autumn oranges and browns, meadowland greens and yellows, or lakeside greens and blues. And colors chosen to re-create nature can be most any combination; even colors we sometimes consider clashing are found harmoniously side by side in a flower.

There is one word of caution about selecting colors. One color can change the appearance of another. For example, a medium green yarn can look quite differently on olive green fabric than it does on white fabric. A blue yarn will change hue under fluorescent lighting as compared to natural lighting. And a bold red may become washed out when placed next to a vivid hot pink.

Thus, when creating a design, it is recommended that you lay the yarn on the fabric with other yarn colors under natural lighting to see whether or not a particular colored yarn will look well.

"Sunset Ship" was selected to illustrate a pleasing design based upon careful selection of shapes, texture, and color. Designer Adele Veres made the ship much smaller in proportion to the open door to give you the feeling of actually standing on the threshold. She selected mostly straight stitches and split stitches to re-create the surface of wood and faraway sky. Her colors are warm brown, yellows, and oranges on gold fabric—a natural scheme we enjoy at sunset and in autumn. "Sunset Ship" is one of the most beautiful and popular designs in the United States today. You, too, can create impressive stitchery by remembering to let Mother Nature be your guide.

FREE-FORM DESIGNING

Another challenging stitchery technique is free-form designing. Here stitchery truly becomes an art form because no patterns are used. You create a mood or impression by your choice of fabric, yarns, and stitches. Perhaps free-form designing is the most exciting aspect of stitchery because there are no absolute rules. Your imagination is your guide and experimentation is the magic word.

Free-form designing is not difficult. But preparation is important. For example, you should allow yourself several uninterrupted hours. (A jangling phone or crying child can really squash your creative mood.)

"Sunset Ship" designed by Adele Veres for Paragon Needlecraft. Available in kit form at department and art needlework stores.

You should have all needed materials within reach. (If the design requires heavy rug yarn and you have to turn the house upside down to find it, again you have interrupted the creative process.) And you should place the fabric in a stretcher or needlework stand. (A hoop would isolate one section at a time, whereas a stretcher or stand allows you to see the whole effect.)

When all these preparations have been made, you are now ready to begin a free-form design. Think of yourself as an artist. The fabric is your canvas. Your needle is your brush. And the yarn is your artist's oil.

Because free-form designing is such an individual art (no two persons will choose the same fabric, yarn variety, or shapes), it is impossible to give specific instructions. However, here are four techniques that may help to get your imaginative juices flowing.

1. *Follow the string technique.* Drop a string or thread on your fabric and follow its suggested shape as your free-form design. You may wish to drop the string once or several times, depending upon the size of your fabric. On the pillow shown, the stitcher used the string technique on green wool with white crewel yarn and linked stitches.

2. *Appliqué a shape technique.* Cut a piece of another fabric in a pleasing shape and machine or hand stitch it to the main fabric. Then use a variety of stitches and yarns to contrast or harmonize with the appliquéd shape. On the example shown, the stitcher selected oranges and yellows for her stitches and fabrics and added even more texture by stitching over marbles.

3. *Vary a stitch technique.* In normal stitchery, stitches are usually evenly spaced, picking up the same amount of fabric each time. But free-form designing offers the opportunity to vary stitch length and to weave, twist, and turn yarn in any shape desired. On the free-form sampler shown, the stitcher worked 24 different stitches in unusual patterns (using circles as a base) to create a design. Notice the pleasing result when the chevron stitch is varied in length, and the clever effect of an unfinished spider web stitch.

4. *Combine with other crafts technique.* If you are adept at another craft, try combining this skill with stitchery. For example, you may attach free crochet onto fabric with the couching stitch. In "Lichen" the stitcher selected brown and gold yarns attached to gold velvet fabric and accented the crochet with French knots. In "Jute Aquarium" the stitcher combined her talents at macramé with stitchery and enhanced her stitches by the addition of tiny beads. In "Swallows" the stitcher used needle and various colored embroidery threads to duplicate string art.

By employing one or all the above techniques, you too will create free-form designs. As stated earlier, experimentation is an important part of free-form designing. Try unusual fabrics. Vary your yarn selection (remember you can also use string, thread, raffia, etc.). Change or invent stitches. You are limited only by your imagination!

By experimenting (and practicing!), you will eventually be able to create a free-form design as stunning as "Crosscut Mandala," which features a wide variety of stitches, appliquéd materials, and yarns of various weights and textures. The creator, Lola Suter, was inspired by studying the cut ends of logs while following logging trucks along the Pacific Coast highways. Her art has resulted in many state and national awards, and she has exhibited her work at the E. B. Crocker Art Gallery in Sacramento.

Tote bag by B. Kay Fraser.

Turtle sampler pillow by Mary Ellen Harris.

Girl's blue jeans by Janet M. Becker.

"Don't Bug Me, Baby" by Lorrie Trano.

"Pigeons' Paradise" by Lorrie Trano.

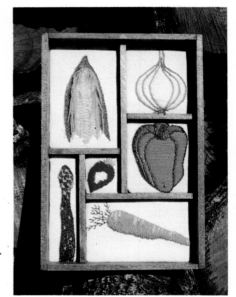

Vegetable ecology box by B. Kay Fraser.

Vest and blouse with Indian design.

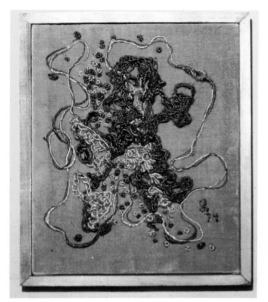

"Lichen" by Gayle Decker.

"Queen Anne's Lace" by LeeWards Creative Crafts, Inc.

"Wheat Field" by Lois M. Smith.

Appliqué with free-form stitching by Mary Ellen Harris.

"Sunset Ship" designed by Adele Veres for Paragon Needlecraft.

Dress by Sherri Gorman.

"Flappin' Turtle" crewelpoint design by SOO-Z.

"Sunburst Flower" by Lorrie Trano.

Girl's scarf and purse sets.

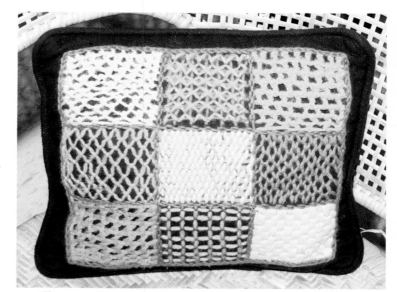

Sampler pillow by Norma J. Evans.

"Wild Nosegay" pillow by Bucilla Creative Needlecraft.

Flower sampler pillow by Janet M. Becker.

"Fuzzy Teddy" designs by Charlene Gerrish for Sunset Designs.

Mushroom picture by B. Kay Fraser.

Snail sampler by Gayle Decker.

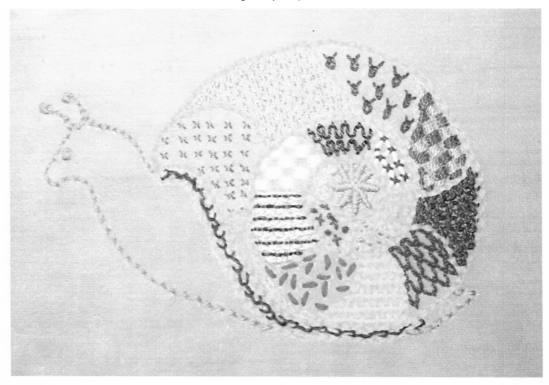

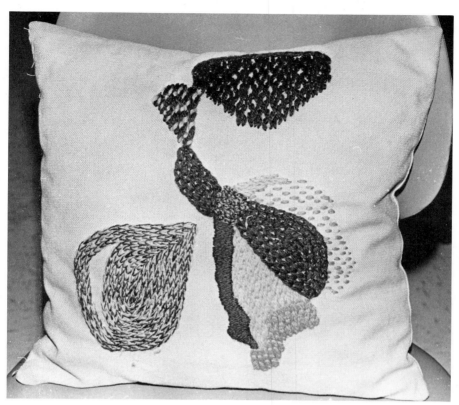

Free-form pillow by Libby Masarie.

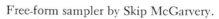

Free-form sampler by Skip McGarvery.

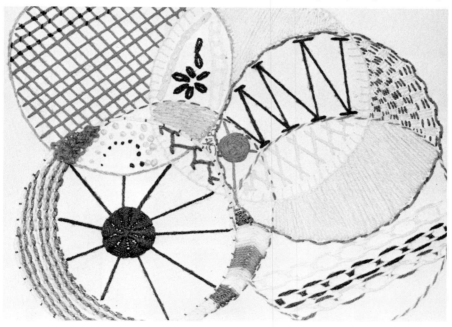

"Jute Aquarium" by Janet M. Becker.

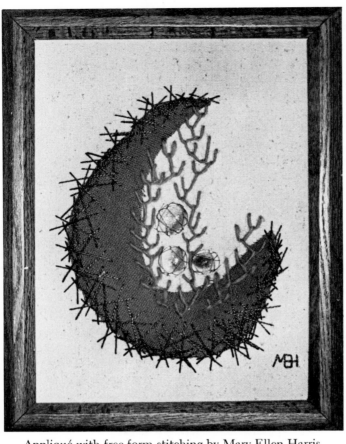

Appliqué with free-form stitching by Mary Ellen Harris.

"Crosscut Mandala" by Lola Suter.

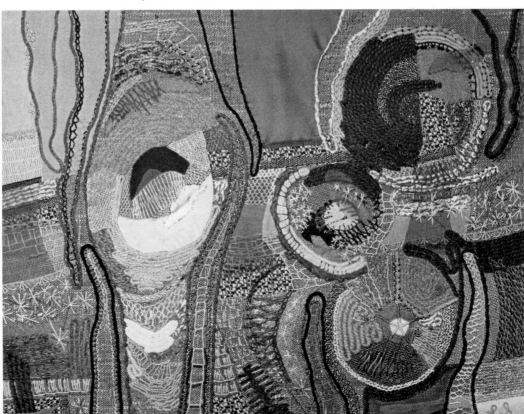

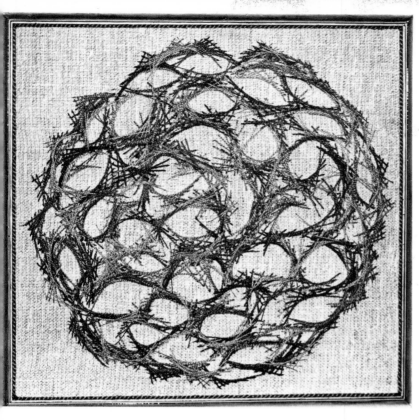

"Swallows" by
Mary Ellen Harris.

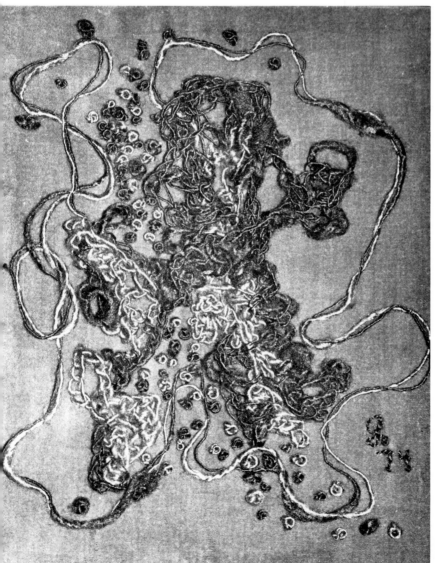

"Lichen" by Gayle
Decker.

EIGHT

STITCHERY... PRETTY AND PRACTICAL

We have discussed earlier that anything you can see, you can stitch. Now let us go one step farther. Any fabric you can see, you can stitch on! In other words, stitchery need not be confined to beautiful wall hangings. With needle and yarn (or thread) you can add stitchery designs to dresses, pillows, neckties, jewelry, blue jeans, doorstops, toaster covers, bookmarks, chair covers, draperies, anything made of fabric.

Thus, stitchery can be not only pretty but practical!

CREATE ON CLOTHING

Ready-made clothing. A clever way to display your stitchery skills is to add designs to ready-made clothing. In fact, embroidered shirts and blue jeans are found in the most expensive boutiques. But you can duplicate these costly designs for pennies.

Place the pattern where desired on the clothing. Use pins or masking tape to keep it in place. Insert dressmaker's carbon paper (sticky side down) under the pattern and trace with a pencil. This transfers the design to fabric. You may also draw the design directly on the fabric with a pencil; stitch freehand; or use iron-on embroidery transfers from the variety store or department store.

Stitchery can transform blue work shirts into expensive-looking designer clothing.

Youngster's blue jeans by Janet M. Becker.

Remember to use yarn or thread that complements the fabric. For example, if the fabric is washable, use washable yarn. If the fabric is tightly woven, use embroidery floss instead of yarn so that fabric will not pucker. A wooden screw-type embroidery hoop is recommended to keep the fabric taut during the stitching process.

Stitchery also provides an economical method to recycle old clothes that are worn or outdated. If a hole has worn in the knee of children's blue jeans, for instance, stitch a design on an iron-on patch and it will last for months. If a dress is no longer fashionable, add stitchery designs and you will be in vogue again. If you dislike a smock or apron because it isn't "you," then add designs that show your individuality. If you want to advertise your business or profession, stitch designs that illustrate your name and trade.

Obviously there is no limit to the way you can enhance ready-made clothing with stitchery. To stimulate your imagination, the following pages show how other stitchers have created on clothing, including some of their patterns.

Popular stitchery patterns for ready-made clothing.

A caftan, handmade in Mexico, shows the stunning effect of simple stitched shapes on dramatic black. By El Palomar de Guadalajara, S.A.

Colorful yarn flowers brought this dress out of the closet and into the fashion spotlight. By Sherri Gorman.

A blue work shirt has stitched memories of a favorite vacation resort. By Lois Collie.

Even aprons become chic with clever free-form designs. By Janet M. Becker.

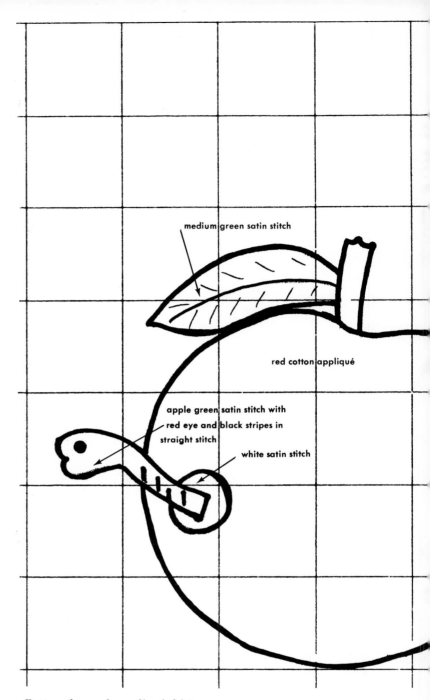

Pattern for apple appliqué shirt.

Appliqué techniques. Another method of decorating ready-made clothing is to combine appliqué designs with stitchery. You fill in a design with another fabric instead of stitches. Appliqué is especially colorful and timesaving on large designs. Here is how to do it.

1. Trace or sketch the design on fabric as usual. Then, using the same pattern, trace the design to be appliquéd on another piece of fabric. On the example shown, the large apple was traced onto red and the smaller apple on green fabric. (Hint: Appliqué fabric should have approximately the same thread count as the original fabric so

stitches will appear evenly on both fabrics.)
2. Cut out the appliqué design with a ¼-inch seam allowance. Machine stitch the seam edge to prevent fraying, then turn the seam allowance under and iron.
3. Pin the appliqué where shown on the design. Attach to the fabric by using tiny blind hand stitches with the same color thread as the appliqué. Iron.
4. Complete the stitched design as usual. The edges of an appliqué design may be enhanced with the blanket stitch.

Appliquéd apples add color and texture to stitchery as well as save time.

A small apple may be stitched on shirt front to coordinate with back design.

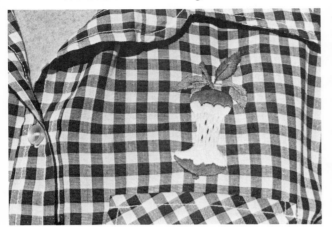

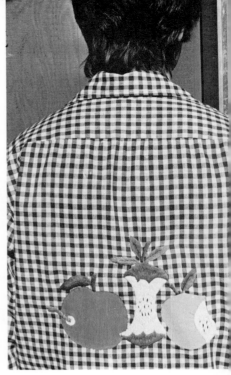

Perk up patterns. Although stitching ready-made clothing is fun and easy, do not overlook the satisfaction of creating the entire garment. Purchase a clothing pattern and fabric from a department store or fabric shop and start from scratch.

Select fabric that is preshrunk or wash before cutting and avoid stretchy fabrics (such as double knits) because your stitchery will be pulled out of shape. Plain colored white and pastel cottons lend themselves well to stitchery.

Select a pattern with simple lines so the garment will not compete with the stitchery. Traditional folk garments, such as peasant blouses,

Mexican folk blouse.

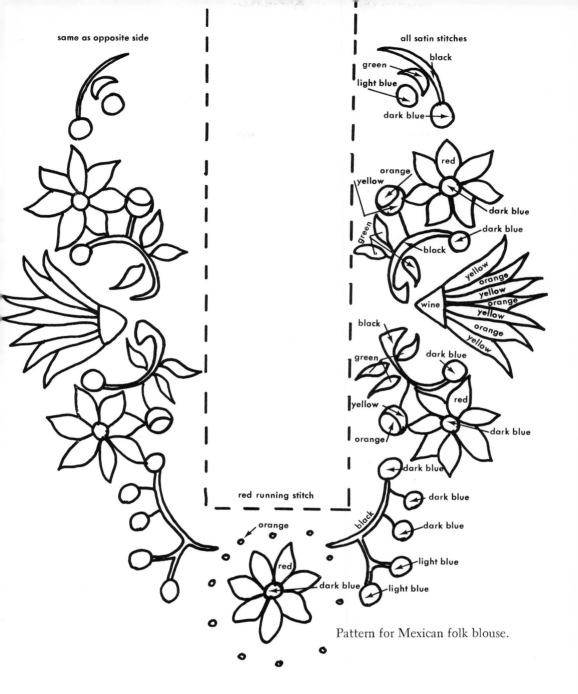

same as opposite side

all satin stitches

black
green
light blue
dark blue

red
orange
yellow
dark blue
dark blue
black
green
wine
yellow
orange
yellow
orange
yellow
orange
yellow

black
green
dark blue
yellow
red
orange
dark blue

dark blue
dark blue
black
dark blue
light blue

red running stitch

orange
red
dark blue
light blue

Pattern for Mexican folk blouse.

are currently in vogue and are stunning with bright colored stitchery. The Mexican folk blouse shown is a good example.

It is usually better to complete the garment before adding stitchery designs so the designs can be placed accurately.

Make up patterns. Still another way to create on clothing is to reverse the design procedure. Normally, you create stitchery designs to enhance ready-made clothing or clothing patterns. But you may also create a clothing design to enhance a stitchery pattern.

As an example, say you are intrigued by an old Indian design that uses accurately placed straight stitches to create shapes. You decide a vest would be an appropriate garment to display such a design. Follow the steps necessary to design any garment:

83

1. Measure yourself. To determine the length of the vest, measure from shoulder center to hipbone. To determine width, measure around back and largest part of chest and add 3 inches for comfort and seam allowance.
2. Make a paper pattern to match your measurements. (You may use a roll of tracing paper, butcher paper, newspaper, etc.) The pattern will vary, depending upon whether front and back are cut separately and the neck design chosen. The easiest method is to make one pattern for both front and back, remembering to divide width in half.
3. Place pattern on doubled fabric with shoulder on fold. Pin in place and cut fabric with ½-inch seam allowance. Remove pattern and cut front straight up the center, branching into a "Y" 6 inches from the shoulder to make a neck opening. (Use a ruler to measure and mark center.) You may trim extra seam allowance from neck opening.
4. Use sewing machine to stay stitch all edges and sew wrong sides together, allowing 9 inches from shoulder for arm opening. Iron seam allowance under on armholes, vest front, and neck opening and hem.
5. Stitch design as usual using wooden embroidery hoop to hold fabric taut. The blanket stitch may be used to finish edges. Bottom fringe may be made by removing cross threads of fabric or with the fringe stitch.

Making up patterns is really quite simple as long as you measure both yourself and the paper pattern accurately. For instance, you can easily turn this vest into a blouse or bathing suit cover-up by eliminating the front cut and making an oval neck opening.

Pattern for Indian design.

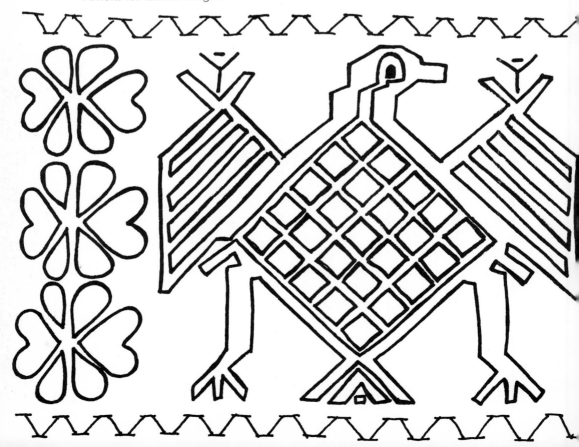

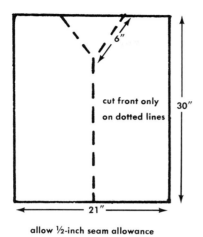

place on fold of fabric

6"

cut front only
on dotted lines

30"

21"

allow ½-inch seam allowance

Pattern for vest.

Fill in design with carefully placed straight stitches.

Vest and blouse with Indian design.

Crewel point "Flappin' Turtle" design by SOO–Z, Box 13761, New Orleans, Louisiana 70185. Available in kit form at art needlework and department stores.

Soft stitchery necklaces by Catherine Mace.

FASHION ACCESSORIES

Even a small amount of stitchery can enhance your appearance and give your wardrobe individuality. Simple designs on jewelry, scarfs, handbags, collars, etc., are quick and easy to do, yet add so much. Here are a few ideas to inspire you.

Jewelry. Stitchery jewelry may be hard or soft. Soft jewelry is made entirely of fabric and hard jewelry also uses metal.

To make soft jewelry: 1) Draw a shape on fabric, such as a circle, heart, triangle, and so forth. 2) Stitch a design within this shape. 3) Cut the shape allowing ¼-inch seam allowance. 4) Cut the same shape for backing; iron seam allowance under; and sew together using tiny blind hand stitches. (You may insert stuffing, such as shredded nylons or bits of foam rubber or cotton balls.) 5) Use heavy yarn, macramé cord, or twine to hang the shape. Attach the cord to the shape with hand stitching or insert the cord between front and back before sewing together. 6) If desired, add fringe or beads to the bottom of the shape.

To make hard jewelry, use an old pendant, necklace, or ring, inserting a stitched design where the old design used to be. Or buy jewelry supplies from the hobby store or lapidary supply store. Then you merely stitch a design on fabric; and secure the fabric to a backing such as stiff cardboard using white glue, masking tape, or stitches. Glue to the metal frame. Kits for stitchery jewelry are also available at art needlework and department stores.

Collars or dickies. Stitchery collars add charm to plain sweaters, blouses, or dresses. To make a collar pattern, trace the neckline of a dress or blouse that fits you well. With the neckline as a base, you can then sketch any desired shape for the collar, such as a square, oval, or point.

Baste or draw the collar pattern on fabric and complete the stitchery before cutting. Then cut with ½-inch seam allowance. Also cut lining for the collar and machine stitch wrong sides together on outside edges. Turn right side out and hand stitch neck side together. Use snaps, hooks, or buttons to fasten.

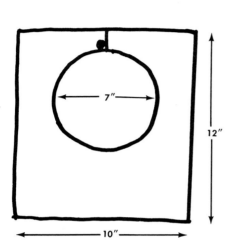

Pattern for stitchery collar.

Stitchery collar by Catherine Mace.

Tote bag. The variety of purses and bags that may be decorated with stitchery is endless. The tote bag shown here was selected because it is easy to make and the size may be varied for use from a small evening bag to a large beach bag. To duplicate the tote bag shown:

1. Cut a paper pattern 12 by 18 inches. Fold pattern in half and draw a curve, which will be the bag's opening. Cut. Unfold and your pattern is complete.
2. You will need to cut two bags from fabric—one for the lining and one for the stitching. On the bag shown, olive green hopsacking was used for the lining and white hopsacking for the stitching. The lining may be cut now, placing the bottom of the bag on the fold of doubled fabric. Cut an extra ½ inch for seam allowance.
3. To prevent raveling, wait until stitching is completed to cut bag from stitchery fabric. However, you may mark fabric with pencil or baste around the pattern to see the shape of the bag.
4. Transfer pattern to stitchery fabric (as explained in Chapter 3) and complete stitchery design. The design shown was inspired by early Jacobean or crewel patterns, and in folk art it is often called a "tree of life" design.

Tote bag by B. Kay Fraser.

5. Cut stitchery fabric as you did the lining with ½-inch seam allowance and place bottom of pattern on fold of fabric.
6. Using a sewing machine, stay stitch all edges of both lining and stitchery fabric to prevent raveling. Then sew sides and top of lining together on wrong side with right sides facing each other. Do not sew curved openings. In the same manner, sew sides and top of stitched fabric.
7. Place the lining inside the stitched bag with wrong sides together. Tuck the seam allowance of curved openings under and pin lining and stitched fabric together. Use tiny blind hand stitches to sew together and remove pins. You are done!

Make your own pattern from paper and pin to fabric.

Pattern for tote bag.

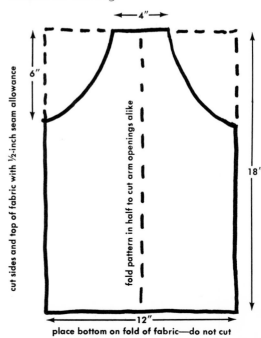

⟵ 4" ⟶

6"

cut sides and top of fabric with ½-inch seam allowance

fold pattern in half to cut arm openings alike

18"

⟵————— 12" —————⟶

place bottom on fold of fabric—do not cut

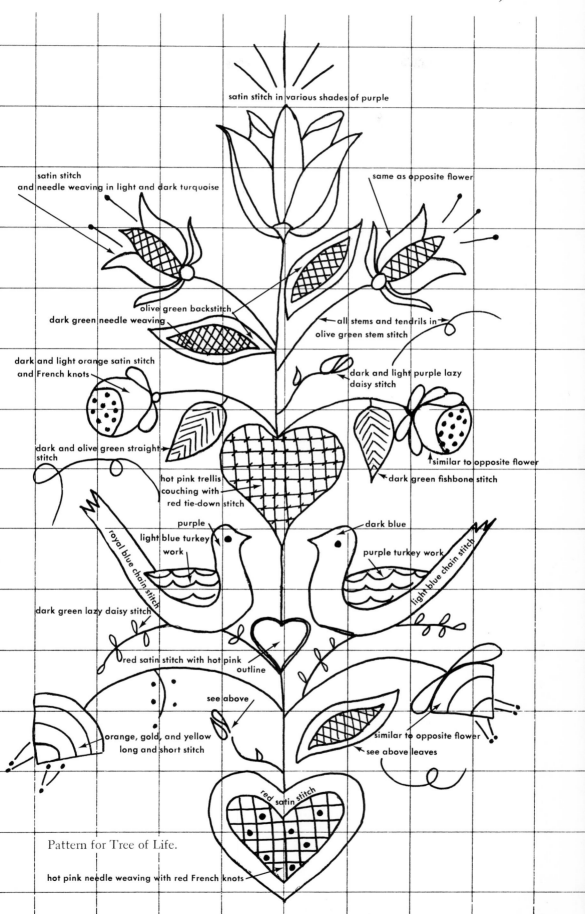

satin stitch in various shades of purple

satin stitch
and needle weaving in light and dark turquoise

same as opposite flower

olive green backstitch

dark green needle weaving

all stems and tendrils in
olive green stem stitch

dark and light orange satin stitch
and French knots

dark and light purple lazy
daisy stitch

dark and olive green straight
stitch

similar to opposite flower

hot pink trellis
couching with
red tie-down stitch

dark green fishbone stitch

purple

dark blue

light blue turkey
work

purple turkey work

royal blue chain stitch

light blue chain stitch

dark green lazy daisy stitch

red satin stitch with hot pink
outline

see above

orange, gold, and yellow
long and short stitch

similar to opposite flower

see above leaves

red satin stitch

Pattern for Tree of Life.

hot pink needle weaving with red French knots

Girl's scarf and purse. Another charming fashion accessory that is sure to delight young girls is a matching scarf and purse set. These sets are so quick and easy to make that young girls can make their own. Here's how.

To make a scarf, cut a 12- by 12-inch square (the size of the square may be adjusted for smaller or larger heads) and stitch a design in one corner. Now fold the square diagonally so the design corner is touching another corner. Turn a ¼-inch seam allowance under and iron. Insert a ribbon or tie made from the same fabric under the fold. Hand or machine stitch sides of scarf together. (If desired, lace may be inserted before stitching.)

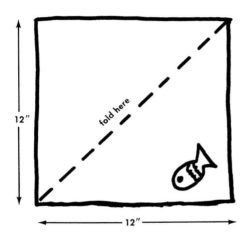 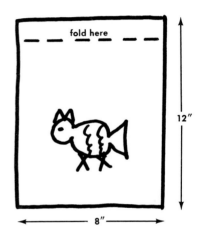

Patterns for scarf and purse.

Girl's scarf and purse sets.

To make the handbag, cut two 8- by 12-inch rectangles. Stitch a design on one of the rectangles. Then, placing right sides together, stitch bottom and sides together. Turn right side out and fold top 1½ inches. Turn unfinished edges under and stitch 1 inch from top. (Or leave edge unfinished and pull cross threads to make a fringe.) Insert ribbon, rope, or fabric drawstrings through the resulting 1-inch channel.

GIFT IDEAS

Friends and loved ones are sure to appreciate small stitched gifts that you can make yourself in an afternoon. In fact, many of the gift ideas shown here are so quick and easy to make that youngsters can also enjoy the stitching fun.

Greeting cards. Colored construction paper and white glue are all you need in addition to normal stitchery supplies to create novel greeting cards in three easy steps:

1. Stitch a small design as usual. (This is a good chance to use scrap fabric and yarn.)
2. Fold the construction paper in half, then fold in half again. This will be your card. On the front of the card, cut a hole large enough for your design to show through. (You may draw a circle, square, or oval, and then cut.) For an unusual effect, the hole may be cut with pinking shears or the edges may be burned by igniting with a match, then quickly blowing out the flame. (Burn a small portion at a time.)
3. Insert the design in the hole and keep it in place by using small amounts of white glue around the edges of the hole on the underneath side.

After the glue dries, you may write your message on the inside. Or, write a short greeting that corresponds with the design. For example, use a snail design and write "I've been slower than a snail about writing." Or, stitch a birthday cake and write "Happy Birthday." The possibilities are endless!

Greeting card designs.

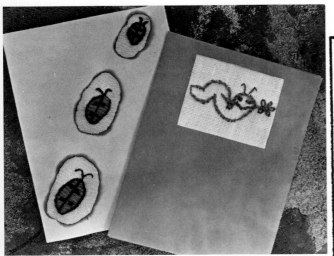

Greeting cards by B. Kay Fraser.

Bookmark by B. Kay Fraser.

medium green blanket stitch (1 strand)

orange long and short stitch (2 strands)

orange yellow satin stitch (2 strands)

yellow loose loop stitch (3 strands)

orange backstitch (1 strand)

good
words
bloom
forever

medium green fishbone stitch (2 strands)

2¼"

Bookmark pattern.

Bookmark. Another quick and easy gift is a bookmark. Decide upon the size of your bookmark, then stitch a design on the fabric before cutting. Cut front (with design) and back. Machine stitch sides and bottom together on wrong side. Turn right side out and hand stitch top. Punch a hole near the top and finish with a buttonhole stitch. Insert yarn in hole.

Many clever bookmark designs are possible, such as a closed eye and the words "This is where I fell asleep." Or, stitch a bright colored worm and the words "Susie is a bookworm." Or, duplicate the design shown, which is sure to please anyone who enjoys books.

Sunglasses case. Since sunglasses are so easy to misplace, friends will appreciate a case that keeps their glasses handy as well as clean. A 3- by 6-inch case should fit most glasses, but allow extra room for extremely large frames.

First, stitch a design to fit the case. Then cut with ¼-inch seam allowance and place bottom on fold of doubled fabric. Use a sewing machine to stay stitch the seam, then sew sides together on wrong side. Turn right side out. Next, cut and sew another case to use as lining. Insert lining in glasses case with wrong sides together. Fold tops under ¼ inch and sew together with tiny hand stitches.

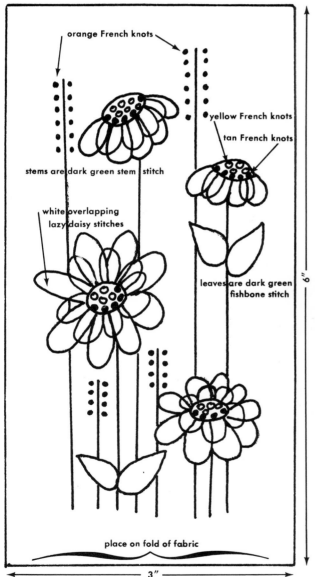

Pattern for sunglasses case.

allow ¼-inch
seam allowance

Sunglasses case by B. Kay Fraser.

Coasters. Novel stitched coasters can be made by purchasing metal and glass frames from art needlework stores or through craft catalogs. Stitch a design to fit the coaster, then cut fabric to fit, and insert in coaster using a cardboard backing. The edges of the fabric may be glued to the cardboard if desired.

Coasters by B. Kay Fraser.

Pattern for coasters.

Pincushion. A handy idea for friends or for yourself is this easy-to-make pincushion that hangs on a chair arm and keeps needles, scissors, etc., ready for use.

First stitch design before cutting so fabric will not fray in hoop. Then cut the following pieces with ¼-inch seam allowance: the main shape (as shown), placing top on the fold of doubled fabric; another main shape for lining, except cut two pieces instead of placing on fold; two pockets; two more pocket pieces to use for lining.

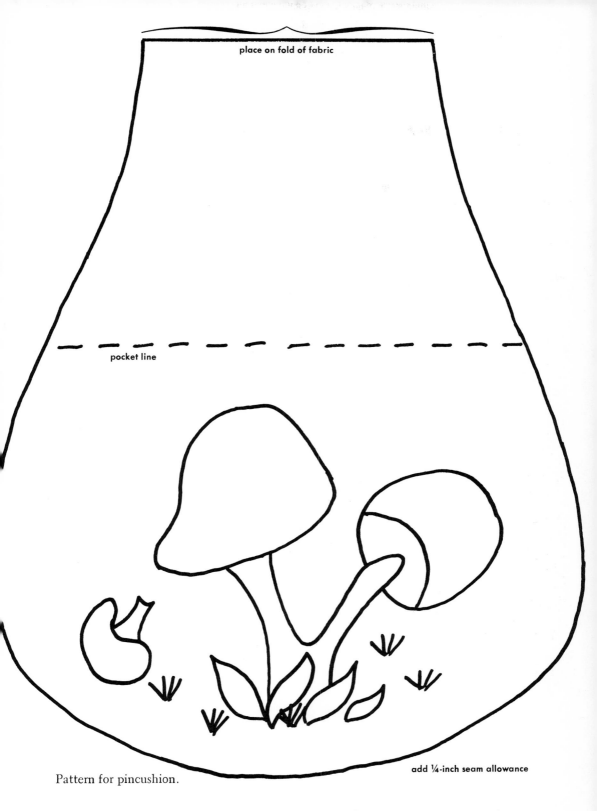

place on fold of fabric

pocket line

add ¼-inch seam allowance

Pattern for pincushion.

Assemble by sewing together on sewing machine. First sew tops of pockets to pocket lining. Then, with right sides up, sew pockets (and lining) to main shape. Next, with wrong sides together, sew lining to main shape. Do not sew the top of the lining yet. Leave this hole open. Pull fabric right side out through the hole.

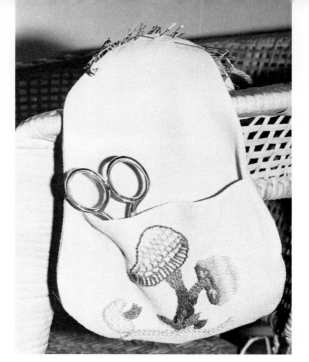

Pincushion by Ruth Chave.

Finally, insert a pincushion (from the dime store) in the hole. (You may leave the small strawberry hanging out the side to sharpen needles.) Now you may sew the lining together underneath, picking up the pincushion fabric with the needle as you stitch to hold in place.

Needle book. Another sewing notion that is pretty and practical is a needle book made of felt. Here's how to make one.

1. Cut four pieces of felt 3 by 4 inches. These are the pages of the book. Cut one piece of felt 3½ by 8½ inches. When folded, this will be the cover to the book.
2. Stitch a free-form design on half of the largest piece of felt. On the needle book shown, the stitcher used several of her favorite stitches, then added the fringe stitch for a border.
3. Fold the large piece of felt over the smaller pieces, with the stitched portion on top. Open and hand or machine stitch pages to cover.

Pieces of felt keep needles handy.

Needle book by Janet M. Becker.

Dust covers. Any household item may be protected from dirt and dust by making a cover enhanced by stitchery. To make a cover, measure, stitch, cut, and sew.

For example, to make a toaster cover, first measure the top and all sides of the toaster. Then draw these measurements on fabric with a pencil and ruler. Draw sides, front, top, and back (or front, top, and back can be one piece). Stitch a design on the front. Then cut all pieces with ½-inch seam allowance. Use a sewing machine to stitch together. Turn bottom under and hem.

You may follow the same principles to make any kind of cover. For instance, make a telephone book cover by measuring the book and allowing an extra 4 inches for an inside pocket to tuck the book cover in. Or, make a doorstop by using a brick or six-inch piece of a 4 by 4. Simply measure, stitch, cut fabric for all sides, and sew fabric together leaving one end open. Insert brick or wood and hand stitch the endpiece.

If preferred, you may sew the cover first, then add stitchery that has been done on another piece of fabric. In fact, this is an excellent method to recycle stitchery. If a blouse or scarf has become worn but the stitchery is still in good shape, then cut out the stitchery and sew it to a dust cover.

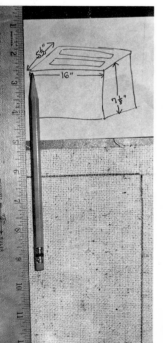

Measure, stitch, cut, and sew to create a cover for any household object.

Toaster cover with recycled stitchery design.

Patterns for Christmas.

CHRISTMAS IDEAS

Christmas is a wonderful time to share your stitchery skills with friends—both as decorations in your home and as gifts to them.

The Christmas hanging shown is easily made by stitching simple designs on felt. Cut felt in a circle and glue to cardboard. When glue dries, glue to 3-inch wooden curtain rings. Finally, add decorative hooks and glue or staple to a wide velvet ribbon.

Here are several other ideas for Christmas giving:

Tablecloths or place mats. Buy or make plain colored tablecloths or place mats, then add Christmas designs with stitchery. These will be perfect for holiday entertaining.

Christmas cards. Follow instructions shown earlier in this chapter for making greeting cards. Substitute Christmas designs.

Tree decorations. Stitch Christmas designs on fabric and insert in wooden curtain rings (as shown) to hang on tree. Or, use felt for stitchery and glue to cardboard for stiffening. (Cover both sides with felt.) Punch a hole in the top to insert yarn for hanging.

Wall hangings. Stitch a large wall hanging of a Christmas scene such as an elaborate wreath, nativity scene, or snowfall landscape. Christmas cards are an excellent source of patterns for wall hangings.

Christmas stockings. Buy or make a Christmas stocking, then enhance it with stitched Christmas designs, a child's name, and perhaps beads and appliqué. Felt may be used.

Christmas hanging by B. Kay Fraser.

MEMORY PLAQUES

Anniversaries, weddings, and births provide the opportunity to stitch the most cherished gift—a memory plaque. These plaques are easily made by following the four basic steps given in the beginning of this book.

Select a design that fits the occasion (greeting cards are an excellent source of design ideas). For example, use fuzzy animal designs on a plaque for a new baby; orange blossom designs on a wedding plaque, etc. Allow space in the center (or where desired) to stitch the names, dates, and so forth. Use small stem stitches or split stitches for lettering.

Still another method of making a memory plaque is to use a birth or wedding announcement or photograph of the couple or baby and stitch around it. Decide where the announcement or photograph will appear on the fabric and place pins or baste stitch this area. Then stitch the surrounding design as usual. When stitching is complete, use white glue to affix the announcement or photograph to the fabric. If desired, you may use a very sharp needle to blanket stitch the edge of an announcement.

Memory plaques may also be used to commemorate any special occasion. For example, when a friend or relative graduates from dental school, stitch a plaque with his or her name, date, graduating institution, and a giant tooth! Or, when a friend's dog wins a field trail championship or a horse wins a race, stitch an animal design along with its name, date, and competition. Even first prize in the pickle canning competition at a county fair calls for a wall hanging with name, date, and pickle!

In this space, glue wedding announcement or photograph of married couple. Or, stitch names, date, and place of marriage using tiny stem stitches or split stitch.

Pattern for memory plaque based on tole design by Carolyn Nordahl.

Memory plaque.

PILLOWS

Another pretty and practical idea for stitchery is to make a pillow. Pillows may be purchased in kit form from art needlework shops or you can easily make your own in three easy steps with any fabric suitable for stitchery.

1. Select a pillow shape and size, then draw the shape on fabric using pencil and ruler for squares and rectangles. For example, if you want a 16-inch square pillow, draw a square on the fabric with each side 16 inches long. To get a circle shape, use a compass or draw around a dinner plate, a round wastebasket, or any other round object that is the size you desire. Cut two pieces of fabric (front and back) allowing ½ inch for the seam. Machine stitch the edges to prevent fraying.
2. Stitch a design as learned earlier in this book. Remember to use washable yarn on washable fabric.
3. Machine stitch front and back together on wrong sides, leaving at least a 6-inch opening to pull right side of pillow out. Stuff with foam rubber, feathers, old nylons, etc., and hand stitch the opening. If you use a ready-made pillow form or piece of solid foam rubber, leave a larger opening for the form to fit through.

Suggested stitches for completing design are: leaves—fishbone stitch; ribbon—stem stitch using darker color where ribbon turns to contrast with lighter shade of upward ribbon; flower petals—satin stitch outlined in darker color stem stitch; and flower center in French knots. By B. Kay Fraser.

Although the above three steps are quick and easy, you may be more pleased with your pillow if you take a few extra minutes to add piping around the edges. Sandwich the piping between front and back sides when you machine stitch the edges. (Use a zipper or cording foot on the machine when sewing piping.) Also, the addition of a zipper so that the filling may be removed for cleaning will be handy. The pillow will stay clean longer by using a spray-on fabric protector (available in the laundry section of the grocery store).

The following photographs show a variety of pillow styles and design ideas. See what you can make!

"Wild Nosegay" pillow by Bucilla Creative Needlecraft. Available in kit form (#1717) at art needlework and department stores.

"Autumn Grain" pillow by Dolly Chambers.

"Spider Web" pillow by Janet M. Becker.

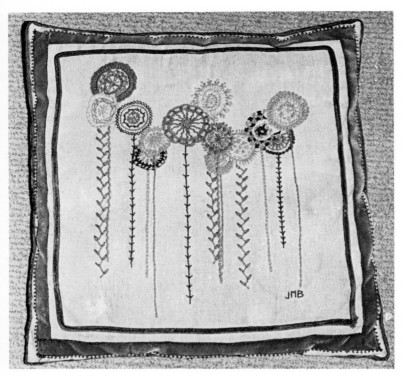

"Flower Sampler" pillow by Janet M. Becker.

"Rosemahling" pillow by Shirley Richards.

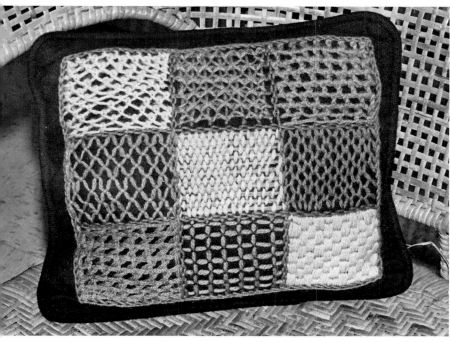

"Sampler" pillow by Norma J. Evans.

"Butterfly" pillow by Norma J. Evans.

INDEX

Pages in italics indicate illustrations